The Agency Blueprint

How to grow your agency business - today, tomorrow…forever.

GW00482146

By Ryan Stewart

Managing Partner, The Blueprint Training

Scan for FREE templates!

Contents

Intro

I've started this book multiple times, always hitting a wall. Once, I tried to outsource it. That too fell flat. Their words lacked my voice, my passion. I had a wealth of experiences and insights to share, but how do you condense a journey of a lifetime into words?

In the meantime, my business expanded, as did my family. Time became a luxury, pushing me towards videos—they were efficient, quicker to produce, yet still impactful. But in my heart, I never let go of this book—the one that tells all.

When I recently found out my wife was pregnant with our first child, something inside of me changed. I realized I have a lot less time than I think, and I would never have more time than I do right now. To make the most of our final year before becoming parents, we planned a month-long trip across Europe, just the two of us.

I set a rule for myself: *no work.* I've been running three businesses and managing a large team, the burnout was real. This trip was about disconnecting and enjoying some personal time before the next big chapter.

One morning in Switzerland, I stared at the incredible Swiss mountains from our hotel balcony. The rising sun lit the peaks, and the view was endless. I took a sip of coffee. The world felt vast, and suddenly, everything clicked. An overwhelming sense of purpose found me right there.

I feel an obligation to put this information out into the world because I know it will help so many people. For most of you, building an agency is incredibly hard.

You're working 70+ hours a week and are still behind. You're living under constant pressure to get results for your clients. You're dealing with staff headaches and turnover. You're not taking home nearly as much income as you should.

I know all of this too well. How? Because that was once me. I used to be overworked and underpaid, trying to figure out if running an agency was really what I should be doing with my life.

But that hasn't been my life for a half a decade now.

I haven't dealt with or done client work in years. I have a small, amazing team of people who have been working with me for 6+ years. My businesses generate 8 figures per year and I make more money than I thought was possible from them. I am not required to work on a daily basis, and I usually work less than 10 hours/week on the agency business.

While I think money is incredibly important (especially in today's increasingly expensive world), I don't want to reduce the information in this book to some get-rich-quick scheme.

This book is about so much more than that. It's about creating a sustainable business model that will bear fruit for years. It's about building a business that you're proud of. It's about building a business that will give you the freedom to do the things that really matter in life—raise a family, travel, create an impact, and experience the world the way God intended us to.

This book is unconventional by the standards of most people. When I sat down to publish it, they told me it was too short. They told me to go write another 500 pages so it will rank better in Amazon's algorithm.

I didn't listen because it's not about "them", this book is about **you**.

I know you're busy. I don't want to jam a 2,000-page book down your throat because I know you will never read it. The most important thing to me is that you actually consume, digest and take action on the words written here.

This is an operating manual for success. I want you to download this information as quickly and succinctly as possible.

There are a ton of resources that I couldn't include inside the printed version of this book, but I've made them available to you online. You can claim them for free, just head to theagencyblueprintbook.com.

At that website, you will find workbooks, templates and a community where you can ask me questions directly.

I hope to see you inside.

P.S. I know how difficult it is to find the time these days to go through an entire book, so I want to leave you with some testimonials from our private Slack community of agency owners just like yourself who have put into action the teaching of this book. Hopefully it will inspire you to push through and take action yourself.

Ryan

Tessah 10:32 AM
Platinum Fam, please allow me to share that I hit $11K for this month!!! I just got off the call with a prospect, and I closed her using my new offering from the Platinum coaching. $7,500! Whaaa!

She's paying tomorrow. She is the third client I closed for August!

 Dan Charles 6 hours ago
I've been doing SEO and PPC for years. Running my own startup. I can safely say that the Blueprint has been invaluable at getting more consistency, improving profitability, delivering a better service and the value the BPT team provide just crushes it imo. I'm.onlynesrly doors on BPT too, but damn, it gives you a level of confidence to really scale your biz. 👍

 Austin Cline 3:10 PM
Hey guys.. this not a showoff post or humblebrag at all. Just a thankful shoutout to @Ryan Stewart and the entire Blueprint team. We just closed an SEO deal with a large home improvement chain, and I used the tools and ideas from Blueprint during the entire process (onboarding, sale, kickoff, budget, audit, etc.) They signed a $70,000 deal yesterday.

So, thank you. You've made a huge impact to my company, my family, and our employees. During this pandemic we've closed more SEO deals than all of 2019, and I credit it to hard work and following this program. (edited)

 ❤7 👍2 🎉1 😊

 6 replies   Last reply today at 4:27 PM

 Sebastiaan Kahle 6 hours ago
The BPT is the total package. Not only how to do SEO the right way but also how to find, attract and close leads. Had the same questions and last month I closed my first blueprint client.

🙌2 😊

 Grant Higginson 7:45 PM
Hey Ryan, signed up for the Blueprint a few days ago and just closed an 80k/year SEM contract using some of your onboarding SOP documents. Looking forward to starting/finishing the rest of the course (edited)

These are just a few of HUNDREDS of testimonials. You can find more at: https://theblueprint.training/reviews/

The History, The Future

To know where we're going, it helps to know where we've been. To fully understand this, I want to go all the way back.

I mean alllllll the way back, to the beginning of civilizations.

Marketing is not a new concept

One of my favorite historical anecdotes is about a merchant in Mesopotamia. This merchant, realizing he was just one among many selling similar products, decided to carve his own unique symbol on his goods, probably one of the first instances of branding.

Marketing is not a new concept. According to a study by Dr David Wengrow, humans began marketing products as early as 5,000 years ago. Sealed caps and marked bottle stoppers became the signs of the origins and quality of a product. These logos essentially served the same function that logos serve for us today, allowing consumers to identify trusted goods.

As civilizations grew more advanced, commerce flourished. Most vendors were simple farmers, artisans, and craftsmen who needed outside experts (the ancient equivalent of "consultants") to help them navigate their growing markets.

And with the birth of capitalist societies, the dynamics changed. Businesses shifted from just selling goods that the market needed (satisfying demand), to selling goods that the market needed (creating demand).

Now businesses were looking for help getting their products/goods/services in front of as many people as possible. And thus, the agency was born.

Agencies are not a new concept, either

Think back to 18th-century London. The streets were likely plastered with posters and flyers, all promoting various goods. Behind a good number of these was William Taylor. He wasn't just posting up random advertisements; he was pioneering the very concept of getting the word out in style.

William Taylor set up shop in London in 1786, marking the birth of what we'd recognize today as an advertising agency. His mission? To help clients get their messages out there, specifically using print media in local newspapers.

Move the clock forward, and radio and television came into play, presenting businesses with incredible opportunities to reach broader audiences. The catch? These mediums didn't come cheap. They were the big leagues, typically reserved for the businesses with the deepest pockets.

Then along came a game-changer: the internet or, as many fondly dubbed it, "Web 1.0." No longer were businesses bound by hefty broadcasting fees. With search engines, chat forums, and email marketing, the doors were flung wide open, allowing businesses to reach new customers on a global scale without draining their budgets.

And just when you thought it couldn't get any more revolutionary, enter "Web 2.0" with the rise of social media. Suddenly, everyone had a voice. With just a smartphone, anyone could engage and reach new customers. It wasn't just about big budgets anymore; it was about big ideas.

The current market for agencies

The last 10 years we've seen a huge increase in digital agencies (with over 400,000 currently in existence) as there has never been more need for our services. There's so much to do when it comes to digital marketing and advertising, making it incredibly difficult to manage it all in-house: SEO, PPC, social media, video marketing, content marketing - the list goes on.

Agencies have stepped in to help businesses of all sizes maximize their digital presence. Through strategic planning, creative content development and careful execution, they have been able to drive results that would have otherwise been impossible.

But it's not just full-blown agencies that are answering the call. As businesses scramble to harness the power of digital, they're often unsure whether they need a guide or a workhorse. This has paved the way for a surge in freelancers and independent experts, creating a spectrum of service offerings. Understanding the difference is crucial, as it directly impacts the strategy and execution of a company's digital initiatives.

Consultants operate in the *knowledge* business. When businesses need help solving complex problems, they hire a consultant to work with them and show them the way (*i.e. "how can we enter a new market"*).

Agencies operate in the *managed services* business. When businesses need help with large projects, they hire an agency to handle it for them (*i.e. "we need a new online brand and website"*).

When you hire a consultant, you enlist them to bring advice and guidance, which you and your team use when executing your marketing. When you hire an agency, you enlist them to do marketing on behalf of your company.

Freelancers have emerged for a couple of reasons. First, work overflow. There are certain types of work that are too small for agencies to handle and too hands-on for a consultant. Second, full-time employees are expensive and a large commitment for companies. Freelancers are project-based or hourly, allowing companies flexibility to get the work done without the long-term commitment.

However, despite all the demand for our services, we're heading into a new age - Web 3.0.

The future for agencies

The blockchain, decentralization, AI...This will change the way businesses approach marketing and advertising, and it has agencies who operate in Web 2.0 extremely nervous.

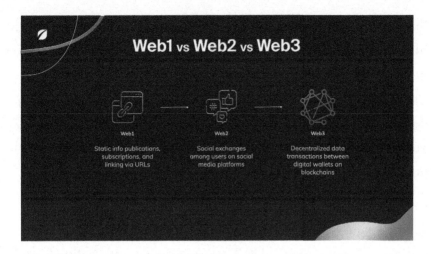

But…don't be. None of these things matter.

Web 1, Web 2, Web 3.

SEO, PPC, email marketing, newspaper ads, TV/radio spots, billboards, metaverse ads, influencers.

These are semantics. These are tactics that will come and go wherever humans are paying attention. What remains consistent is the human need for connection, storytelling, and trust.

Your job is **not** to sell a service. Your job is to help your clients get more customers.

How you get them more customers should always be the fastest, most profitable way to do so. Most of you are romantic about the service you provide, so you force it on clients, even though it's not what's best for them.

If you are romantic about the service you provide, you are already out of business - you just don't know it yet.

Period. End of story. Mic drop.

I'm looking at you, SEO professionals. I've been working in the SEO industry for nearly 15 years - it's mind-blowing to me how many of you are willing to go down on a sinking ship.

Most of you have been doing the exact same thing for almost a decade, even though the world is changing in front of your eyes. Your job is to sell the service that's going to get results quickly, profitably and scalably.

Is SEO still a good way to do that? For some businesses, yes.

But most of you are jamming that service down the throats of businesses who don't need it. That's why you are struggling to grow. You're selling sand to the beach. No, you're selling sand to a bowling alley. They don't want it, they don't need it.

If you are not directly helping a business grow, you are wasting your time.

But look - I get it. You've spent 10 years learning and perfecting how to do SEO (or Instagram marketing, Meta Ads, etc.).

I'm not telling you to stop learning about the tactics. I'm telling you to focus on the highest-impact tactics for your clients, not the tactics you think are best. If you don't, you will get gobbled up by what's coming in the future.

What you should do right now

Why did I just give you a history lesson?

Because I want to give you comfort that *you are on the right track.*

So many agencies that I work with have anxiety about the future.

> *"Is AI coming for my business?"*

"How much time do we have left running an agency?"

"Is it really worth it to start an agency business?"

I wanted to go all the way back in time to show you that this business model has been around for centuries, and it will continue to be for those who are focused on the right things.

What are the "right things"?

Business results for clients. If your agency is focused on making your clients more money, you will make money... Now and forever (no matter what happens with the economy or AI).

Stop selling services, start selling results. The rest of this book will help you get aligned to make sure you're doing so. In the coming chapters, you'll learn how to recalibrate your offerings, connect more deeply with clients, and ensure your agency's longevity.

The Operating Framework

There are all types of agencies - marketing, digital ads, design, development... How can we group them all into a single framework?

Simple. It's not about what you do (us, the agencies), it's about them (your client) and the results they want to see.

You see, your client's success depends on the 'outcome they achieve from working with you'. So everything we do should be focused on helping to increase that outcome - whether it's increased lead generation, more efficient customer onboarding, higher ROI whatever. Too many agencies fail because they forget that (or never knew it to begin with).

They get stuck selling a service that no one wants (I'm looking at you, SEO agencies). You're stubborn, you sell what you know how to do, instead of what the client/market needs.

The only thing that matters is getting results for your clients, aka making them money. This framework ensures that you will always achieve that. You can literally copy and paste this to generate new revenue streams once you master it.

It ensures you will *always* create value in the market, no matter what the world or economy is doing around you.

I call it the 5 Pillar Framework - it breaks down as follows...

1. **Market Positioning**: Find a painful problem to solve for the right client, then build a mechanism (offer) to deliver.

2. **Offer Productization**: Turn your offer into a streamlined machine with processes, people and automation.

3. **Service Mastery**: Become the best in the world at delivering your offer and getting results for your client type.

4. **Client Acquisition**: Attract prospects to your agency with the right messaging on the right platforms.

5. **Sales**: Create an engine to find and close deals at scale.

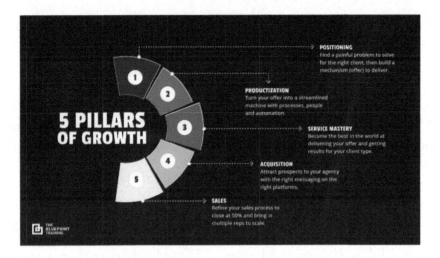

Consider a working with local roofing contractor - under the 5 Pillar Framework:

1. You identify their primary issue - they're not generating enough leads in their local area.

2. You develop an offer specifically for roofing businesses, which includes local SEO and local search ads.

3. You ensure that your team are experts on search marketing for roofing business, and they know the ins and outs of the roofing business.

4. You create targeted content demonstrating your knowledge of roofing marketing, and you post about it regularly on LinkedIn.

5. You fine tune your sales process to close out roofing companies.

I've spent years ideating and refining this framework, both in building my own agency businesses and working with thousands of agencies who have come through The Blueprint Training.

This framework holds true whether you're doing $100/month or $1,000,000/month. The pillars are also organized based on your current revenue benchmarks.

- **Pillar 1: Market Positioning** - $0 to $10k/monthly revenue.
- **Pillar 2: Offer Productization** - $10 to $25k/monthly revenue.
- **Pillar 3: Service Mastery** - $25k to $50k/monthly revenue.
- **Pillar 4: Client Acquisition** - $50 to $100k/monthly revenue.
- **Pillar 5: Sales** - $100k to $250k/monthly revenue.

Now, of course, these are generalizations, actual numbers will vary depending on your location/market. But they are a solid jumping-off point to understand where your focus needs to be based on your current performance.

Each upcoming chapter in this book will break down the 5 Pillars in great detail, along with examples of these pillars in action. Regardless of what your revenue is, I implore you not to skip over a chapter. They are tied together in a symbiotic relationship, skipping over one will change the flow of the book.

The Traditional Agency Model	The Blueprint Agency Model
• Delivers services that are viewed as expenses (easy to cut) • Wasteful ops model - office spaces, tons of people, endless software bills • Never-ending workloads, jack-of-all-trades model • 10% - 20% NET margins (high headache low margin • Commoditized market, race to the bottom pricing • Difficult to attract and close the "right" clients	• Delivers results for clients that become integral to their business • 100% remote, A handful of people with AI • Finite scope work for a singular ICP that is productized • 40% - 60% NET margins (make money) • Competitive market of one, top-of-market pricing • Easy to target and close great clients to work with

Think of the traditional agency model as an old family car. It's reliable and familiar but also bulky and occasionally breaks down. On the other hand, The Blueprint Agency Model is the electric car of the agency world—modern, efficient, and attuned to today's needs.

Traditional agencies often deliver services viewed as expenses, operate on wasteful models, and face the challenge of commoditized markets. The Blueprint model, however, is about delivering undeniable results, operating lean with a focus on remote teams and AI, and creating unique value in the marketplace.

By the end of this book, you'll grasp exactly how to streamline your agency, ensuring it thrives no matter the market's twists and turns.

We'll ditch the 'jack of all trades' mindset. Instead, you'll master laser-focused strategies that resonate with your clients and boost your bottom line.

Whether you're kickstarting an agency or reinvigorating an established one, these pages will be your guide to tangible success.

Let's dive in, and transform your agency game.

PILLAR 1

Market Positioning

A few years ago I was on a 1 on 1 call with a client (let's call her "Hannah"). During our working session, I asked her about her target client. Her eyes lit up and she responded:

"Any business that needs my services!".

It was evident she loved her craft. But beneath that enthusiasm lay a tangled web of misdirection. While she was confident that 'anyone and everyone' was her target audience, she was overwhelmed with frustration because of her inability to attract and retain clients.

It quickly became apparent that Hannah's 'scattergun' approach wasn't getting her anywhere. She was in the same predicament most young agencies find themselves in, "a jack of all trades, but a master of none".

This isn't an isolated incident.

When I start working with a new agency client for 1 on 1 coaching, I always start by asking the same question:

"Who is your target client?"

Most agencies don't have a straight answer to that question.

"Anyone who will pay our retainer".

"It depends".

"Well we do Instagram marketing, so anyone who needs Instagram to grow is a good fit for us".

These are all wrong answers because they are all about "me", and not about "you". We are here to help our clients grow, we are not here to do what is best for us.

When thinking about your "who"...

1. You need to be able to clearly identify who you work with (industry, niche, vertical, etc)

2. You need to create an offer specifically for the type of client you work with.

Put yourself in your client's shoes. And I don't mean a cursory glance. I mean to truly feel the weight of their challenges, the rhythm of their daily operations, and the hopes that light up their entrepreneurial journey. Understand what keeps them up at night.

Many of you are misaligned here. You're trying to force a service offering that's not a good fit for a specific type of business.

This creates a scenario where you're not getting results (aka the client is upset), and you're creating more work for yourself trying to get it to work.

Square peg, round hole. No amount of effort will make it work.

Offer / Market Fit

Ever tried wearing a shoe that's either too tight or too loose? That's what it feels like when there's no what I call Offer / Market fit. Let's understand why this fit is your agency's Cinderella moment.

You've likely heard of Product / Market fit, which is used in the product/software industry.

Product / Market fit refers to the degree to which a product satisfies a strong market demand. It creates a unique product offering that people desperately want.

Product companies spend millions of dollars trying to figure out their Product / Market fit because the success of their company depends on it.

Agencies spend no time on this concept. It becomes a foundational issue and is usually one of the core reasons why you struggle.

Imagine two architects. One carefully studies the terrain, understands the purpose of the building, and designs accordingly. The other just uses a generic blueprint for every plot. Which building do you think stands tall and serves its purpose? The same principle applies to agencies and their Offer / Market fit.

Offer / Market fit refers to the degree to which we are doing the right thing for our client base that MAXIMIZES outcomes, at a price that makes sense.

Mastering Offer / Market fit is how you **ensure your success no matter what** the economic climate is, or AI, or if Google blows up. Mastering Offer / Market fit ensures you are always focused on solving the biggest problem for your target customer, which **will always keep you in high demand**.

When you are in alignment, everything becomes easier:

- **You stand out from the competition**

  The market understands exactly who you help and how you help them. Instead of "being a jack of all trades and a master of none" you are a specialist with a clear value proposition to your target prospects. Over time, clients will literally come to you (and you only) to solve their problems.

- **Daily operations clears up**

  When you work with a single type of client, with a single offer, delivering your service becomes easier (and cheaper). Doing SEO for an ecommerce shop vs SEO for a coffee shop are completely different services, which requires more energy to fulfill.

- **Results flow for clients consistently**

  It's 10,000 times easier getting results when you are focused on solving problems for a singular type of business. Doing the same thing over and over builds repetition and allows you to create systems. Systems allow you to get more consistent results, while improving them over time. It's much easier to build on existing processes than constantly creating new ones (or doing custom work).

- **Hiring is a breeze**

  You no longer need a ton of roles, just a small handful. This makes it much easier (and cheaper) to find talent, because you aren't asking them to be verified experts, you just need them to follow a proven process over and over.

- **Work "on" the business, not "in" it**

  Specializing truly allows you to pull yourself out of the business and focus on 'big rocks'. You will never have to do client work again once you get your offer dialed in.

- **Marketing is simple**

  How can you create marketing messaging when you don't know who you are talking to? Specializing in a single type of client allows you to create targeting marketing campaigns that fills your pipeline on autopilot.

It's not 2012 anymore. You can't service everyone. There's too much to do, and there's too much competition. Specialization is no longer just a strategy; it's a necessity.

And to show you how powerful specialization can be, I'd like to introduce you to one of my clients, Brendan. 5 years ago he was a teacher, with a family to take care of and other obligations, who had a burning desire to make a change. He began looking for alternative ways to generate income, and eventually stumbled across internet marketing and SEO. Soon after he joined our agency training program.

Before joining, Brendan was searching to find consistency in his business, and a steady means to generate income for his family. It wasn't until Brendan realized that he needed to specialize in order to stand out from the competition that his business really began to grow. He had a passion for SaaS and for helping businesses find their unique tone of voice, so he decided to focus on specializing in content SEO for SaaS.

And boy, did it pay off. Within just a few months of deciding to specialize, Brendan was able to double his rates, land bigger clients, and start getting featured in industry publications.

Nowadays, Brendan is one of our top-performing clients. In just a year, his agency reached an incredible milestone, $1 million in annual recurring revenue.

Next, we have Tessa. Tessa was initially offering general SEO services, but found that she wasn't able to scale her business as quickly as she wanted. So, she decided to focus on a specific niche - leveraging Help A Reporter Out (HARO) for backlinks. This decision allowed her to leverage her existing network and knowledge, while also taking advantage of a high demand for this specialized service. Today, she runs a successful team that cranks out high authority backlink campaigns month after month. As a single mom, she is proud to have grown her agency and now she can charge as much as $30,000 in monthly contracts through redefining her offer.

I know you feel like focusing on a single type of client is a step back. In the short term, yes, it will be a step back - but only so you can take 100 steps forward in the right direction.

How to Master Offer / Market Fit

This might feel like assembling a jigsaw puzzle, but bear with me. Once you see the whole picture, you'll wonder how you ever worked without it.

Mastering your Offer / Market fit is a 2-part process:

1. **Market positioning**: Identify a target client with a customer acquisition problem.

2. **Offer creation**: Determine the most effective, profitable, and quickest way to get them more customers.

Let's go through how to do this for your business.

Part 1: Finding your target market positioning

A friend started with a dream of catering to SaaS companies. Bright-eyed, he believed he had the key to their marketing success. But a few months in, he realized he was trying to play a symphony without ever having learned the notes. The intricate nuances of SaaS marketing took him by surprise, leading to a steep learning curve and unsatisfied clients. ....

The best start in identifying "who" your target client should be in places where you have experience. Otherwise, it's difficult to know how to get them results.

For example, a lot of people want to work with SaaS companies, because they are technically savvy and have large marketing budgets. However, SaaS marketing is dramatically different from ecommerce marketing (or local, etc.).

Why?

With SaaS companies, you're generally working with a type of client that is highly informed. They generally have an internal marketing team in place, but they use agencies to fill gaps in their knowledge or to help them scale. If you're just starting an agency and have never worked with a SaaS company, working with them would be like drinking from a firehose.

Every market position will come with a different set of challenges. Part of your job is to learn the ins and outs of your market over time.

- What / how / why do agencies fit into their plan/budget?
- What non-marketing challenges do they face?
- What's happening in their market?

The goal is to become a trusted resource in the eyes of your target market. It's not just about speaking their language; it's about dreaming in it. Dive deep, become an insider, and let your marketing resonate with authenticity.

For example, our agency targets law firms. We spend a lot of time internally educating ourselves on the legal market. We want to learn everything we can about running a law firm so we can speak their language through marketing and sales.

Once you pick a general direction, there are 4 ways for you to hone in on your target.

- Industry

  Industries are very broad so they provide a good starting place for your search. If you are just getting started, this will be too broad and you will need to continue to drill deeper.

  Examples: B2B, SaaS, ecommerce, etc.

- Niche industry

  This would be the traditional "niche" focus you've heard of, likely in a Facebook Group somewhere. It's a subset of an industry that is deeper specified by business type.

  Examples: Coffee shops, crossfit gyms, law firms, home supply stores, etc.

- Platform or technology

  When a company is tied to a complex platform, they need help from agencies or consultants who specialize in working with them. For example, DemandWare is a complex (and expensive) ecommerce platform. If a company is using it, the agency they hire will need to be well-versed in how to use it in order to work with them.

Examples: Shopify, DemandWare, Klaviyo, etc.

- Job function

  Honing in on the specific person you're selling to is a great way to drill deeper into your positioning.

  Examples: Business owner, CEO, marketing teams, etc.

- Revenue range

  Adding revenue to your target client immediately qualifies your market. If you choose this route, make sure to stick to a band that you're comfortable with. If you're just getting started, you should not be targeting businesses that do $10M or more in revenue.

  Examples: startups, SMB, $1,000,000 ecommerce stores

Selecting 1 of the above isn't enough - you need to go deeper. The more you specialize, the more impactful your market position will be.

Did you know that there are over 30,000 SaaS companies worldwide? And yet, the most successful agencies I've seen don't market to 'SaaS companies'. They cater to 'B2B SaaS startups in HR tech below $10M in revenue'. See the difference?

You might be thinking that deeper specialization will cut you off at the knees. In reality, it allows you to charge more.

- SEO agency = $
- SEO for ecommerce = $$
- SEO for Shopify stores = $$$
- SEO for 7-figure Shopify stores = $$$$

The more specific you are, the more targeted your offer becomes. In a study conducted by Databox, an astonishing 80% of agencies identified as niche, and it's no wonder why. Niching offers precision. By becoming an expert in a particular field or service, you can resonate more deeply with a specific segment of clients.

And while it may seem that narrowing your focus limits opportunities, it often does the opposite. When you cater to a specific market, you're better equipped to understand their unique challenges and aspirations.

However, this doesn't mean the generalist approach is obsolete. There's a market for that too. But as you navigate this, remember: it's not about casting the widest net, but about casting it where you're certain the fish are abundant. In a world where agencies are plenty, being relevant to a specific few might just be your golden ticket.

Validating your market

So, you've picked a niche. But is it a gold mine or a minefield? Once you've solidified a position, you need to vet it to make sure it's worth moving forward with.

Consider your chosen market position as a potential partner. Before committing, you'd want to ensure there's compatibility, mutual benefit, and a future, right? The same scrutiny applies here.

You can use these questions to validate your target:

1. **How painful is the problem that needs solving?**

   Remember, your job is to help your target client get more customers. Depending on who you choose, the level of pain may vary. The more painful the problem, the more you can charge.

2. **Is there purchasing power?**

   A lot of businesses need help getting more customers, but not every business can afford to pay for your services. You need to understand how the business works in order to fully answer this question.

3. **Is the client easy to find / target?**

   If you can't easily target the client, it will be really difficult to generate leads for yourself. Think about it this way - can you go onto Facebook Ads and target them? Can you build a list of them on LinkedIn Sales Navigator?

4. **Does the result of your service end up in a conversion?**

   This is the most important question - are you able to get them results? Let's say you want to do SEO for gyms because you love fitness and have experience working in them. You will never be able to make them money because SEO is not an effective way for gyms to get customers. You need to be brutally honest with yourself here, or you will never find success.

5. **How many conversions are needed to pay for your service?**

   What are the unit economics behind making your clients more money? I know that if I work with a roofing company, they need 5 leads to sign 1 client. 1 client is worth $30,000 to them, so as long as I can drive them 5 leads per month they will make 5x on my services.

If you can't do that equation for your target client, it's going to be incredibly more difficult to sell them.

You won't find your target market on the first try. Go through this process multiple times until you find one that sticks.

As you digest the insights from this chapter, remember: every agency's journey is unique, but we all share common milestones. If you're keen to delve deeper and refine your path, consider exploring what The Blueprint Training offers. It's a space filled with resources and tools tailored for agency owners like you. If you wish to delve deeper into these concepts, consider giving it a look. You can find more at: https://theblueprint.training.

Part 2: Defining the perfect offer

Now that you've defined your "who", it's time to define the "what". The "what" = your agency's offer, aka the service you will provide. This is where many agencies either hit a home run or strikeout. Let's ensure you're swinging for the fences.

Remember (for the 100th time), your offer/service should be focused around acquisition for your target client.

So if you're targeting law firms, the result of your service should provide more leads and cases. If you're targeting sports apparel ecommerce stores, the result of your service should drive more store purchases.

When it comes to acquisition, there are two types:

1. **Direct acquisition** - running Pay-per-click call ads for law firms.

2. **Indirect acquisition** - link building for ecommerce stores to improve SEO rankings.

The more your offer is focused on direct acquisition, the better received it will be by your target client.

Offer criteria

The goal here is to put together a service offering that is a "no-brainer" for a prospect. There are a few things to consider that dramatically will increase your success when building an offer.

- **What's the likelihood of results?**

  Is this the absolute best, most effective way to get your target client more customers? Do you think doing Facebook Ads for a coffee shop will deliver them more customers? Do you think doing content marketing for a SaaS company will deliver them more customers?

- **What's the cost?**

  Is there a large cost required to deliver your offer? Is there enough margin left for your target client to make money off of your services?

- **Speed (time to results)**

  Is this the fastest way to get them more customers? No one wants to wait 6 months for results, the faster you can move the needle the more enticing your offer will be.

- **Effort to deliver**

  Do they have to do any work / dedicate resources to help you deliver your offer? Depending on how you deliver your service, you may need the client's help. The more you can take off their plate, the more enticing your offer will be.

- **What's the perceived value?**

  Yes, your job is to sell an outcome that solves an acquisition-based problem. However, there's a big difference between "we can drive more customers" and "we will double your revenue with a customized acquisition strategy." The latter is worth 10x the former, so be sure to frame your offer in terms of value (as opposed to just quantity).

The offer statement

You need to be able to communicate the value of your offer in 1 sentence or less. A simple tool to communicate your offer is an "offer statement".

Consider your offer statement as the tagline of a movie poster. It should be compelling enough to make someone want to buy a ticket and see the whole show. It's the gateway to your agency's blockbuster.

So, your offer statement should be a single sentence that answers 3 key questions:

- Who is it for?
- What do they want?
- How do they get it?

For example...

We help *law firms* (**who**) *get more leads* (**what**) through *blended search marketing campaigns* (**how**).

That simple sentence clearly speaks to the who, what, how of our service offering. It's equivalent to an elevator pitch for agencies. You can use it as a tagline on your website or as a response when someone asks "what do you do".

Crafting your offer

Now, of course, your service offering will be more than a statement. I like to lead with the offer statement because it's a concise way to think about your offer.

However, this will likely be a complex service with multiple moving parts. Let's talk about how you define your service offering in a concise way as well.

A lot of agencies make the mistake of doing too much. They throw a ton of deliverables or action items into a service that simply don't need to be there. If the action doesn't directly impact the growth of your client's business, leave it out. A clear, focused offer will resonate more than a cluttered, all-encompassing one.

This exercise will help you to strip down the fat and focus on the highest impact levers of a service offering. The easiest way for me to teach this is through example. I will be using my agency WEBRIS as an example.

WEBRIS: a search marketing agency for law firms

Step 1 - Identify the dream outcome of your target client

WEBRIS = more qualified consultations

Step 2 - List out all roadblocks stopping your client from achieving their dream outcome

In other words, what is holding back your client from getting more qualified consultations? If you don't know, that's a problem - you need to do more research on your target client / market.

Aim to list out 3 to 5 roadblocks max - anything more will create an offer that is overwhelming and unfocused.

WEBRIS

- *Unoptimized local presence (reviews, GBP, local listings)*

- *Missing key website content to rank for bottom-funnel search queries*

- *Lacking authority to rank for competitive terms due to a lack of links*

- *Unable to find profitable keywords with PPC ads, costing a fortune to get leads*

Step 3 - Turn all problems into solutions that you can manage for your client

Now we simply turn these roadblocks into solutions. These problems will literally become the service that you offer.

WEBRIS

- *Optimize local presence (review outreach, GBP, citations)*

- *Create key website content to rank for bottom-funnel search queries*

- *Acquire links via outreach to build authority and ranking equity*

- *Refocus PPC ads on long tail keywords*

That's it. You now have a service offer you can test in the market.

Yes, it's really that simple - simple is *good.* Simplicity ensures that your offer maps directly to your target client's pain points, which they understand and feel on a daily basis.

You lose prospects when you start getting too complex with your service pillars. Keep in mind, **they don't care about what you can do, they care about themselves.** When you build your offer around their problems, it ensures that you will have their attention throughout the process.

In the next chapter, we will focus on blowing out these bullet points into a full-blown service and project plan, but for now, this is all you need.

Macro vs Micro offers

The final note on offers before we close this chapter, Macro vs Micro offers.

- **Macro offer** - Business offer. This is what we just spent time flushing out. Your Macro offer is the vehicle which begins the exchange of value (business) for dollars (customer). In other words, your Macro offer is your service offering.

- **Micro offer** - Marketing offer. Later in this book (Pillar 4) we will talk about how to generate leads for your agency. A Micro offer is a key part of that process because these are what I like to call marketing offers. A Micro offer is what we use to bring people into our ecosystems with the ultimate goal of selling our Macro offer. To make this easy for you, think ebook, whitepapers, webinars, etc.

We can ideate Micro offers by simply using the roadblocks we just defined during the offer build process. Again, this ensures our marketing material is focused on our target client's problems, as opposed to your service. Focusing on their problems will always ensure your marketing pops and generates engagement.

Let's look at some examples of how my agency WEBRIS tackles this.

- Macro offer =

We help law firms get more leads through blended search marketing campaigns.

- Micro offer(s) =

  - *How to generate 5-star Google Reviews for your law firm*

  - *Building content that attracts leads to your law firm*

  - *How to get your law firm featured in high authority press websites*

We will explore Micro offers in more detail later in the book, I just wanted to lay the foundation here, as everything ties back to your offer.

In the next chapter, we will begin the process of "productizing" your offer into a streamlined, automated delivery machine.

Action Steps for Mastering Market Positioning

Before moving on to the next pillar, let's solidify your understanding and application of Market Positioning. Use the following exercises to draw insights from this chapter and begin shaping your agency's direction.

1. Target Client

Reflect on your existing clientele to gain clarity on your potential target market.

- *Who are your top 3 current clients?*
- *What industries are they in?*
- *What specific challenges do they face?*
- *Why did they choose your agency?*
- *List 3 similarities among these clients.*

2. Offer / Market Fit

Evaluate how well your current services align with your target market.

- *List down the top 3 services you offer.*
- *For each service, who is it best suited for? (Industry, revenue range, business type, etc.)*
- *Is there a mismatch between your target market and your current services? If yes, what adjustments can be made?*

3. Market Positioning

Specialize and refine your market positioning.

- *Select an industry you're interested in. List down specific niches within this industry.*
- *Which platforms or technologies are commonly used within this industry/niche?*
- *Who are the key decision-makers within these businesses? (Job function)*

- *Estimate the average revenue range of these businesses.*

4. Market Validation

Ensure the viability of your chosen market with this validation checklist.

- *How painful is the problem you're solving for this market? Rate from 1 (not painful) to 10 (extremely painful).*

- *Can businesses in this market afford your services? (Yes/No)*

- *List down three platforms or methods to target these businesses.*

- *Does your service result in a conversion for them? (Yes/No/Maybe)*

- *Estimate: How many conversions are needed to pay for your service?*

5. Offer Brainstorming

Craft an offer that resonates with your target market.

- *Describe the target client (niche, platform, revenue, etc.).*

- *List down their top 3 challenges.*

- *How can your agency address each challenge?*

- *Draft a concise offer statement incorporating the solutions.*

6. Macro vs Micro Offers

Test out different offers targeting the same niche.

- *Elaborate on your agency's Macro offer (your primary service offering).*

- *Brainstorm 3 Micro offers (marketing offers) that can pique the interest of potential clients and address their pain points.*

Head to theagencyblueprintbook.com to claim your FREE workbooks.

PILLAR 2

Offer Productization

One of the biggest knocks on the agency business model is the amount of time, energy and stress it takes to deliver the services. 80-hour weeks, non-stop demand from clients, constantly stuck working on deliverables...most people burn out pretty quickly.

I remember a time when we had a major client project due, and we were juggling numerous tasks, not entirely sure if we'd complete everything in time. This chaos was a wake-up call.

What's the solution?

Standardization. Systems. Processes. Turning your complex service into a streamlined assembly line.

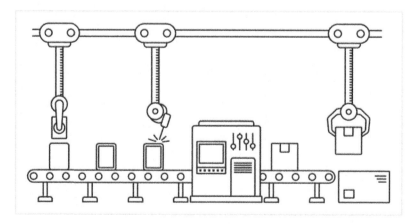

Standardization ensures uniformity, systems help in automating repetitive tasks, and processes act as a guide for the team to follow, ensuring every project is handled with the same level of excellence.

I like to call this "Offer Productization". While I didn't invent the term, I do like to think I've been a big part of bringing this concept to the agency world.

"Productizing" a service is the process of documenting processes that can be run (without customization) to achieve a promised business result. It can be run with a standardized labor force (or automation) without your direct involvement.

A productized service is the only path to pulling yourself out of your agency's operations. This can only be achieved with a clearly defined Market Positioning (Pillar 1). If you are trying to do everything for everyone, it's impossible to create the systems needed to productize.

Why Productize?

Have you ever felt overwhelmed by the sheer variety of tasks in an agency project? Enter the concept of productization.

This is a foreign concept for a lot of you and likely goes against the grain of what you have always thought an agency should be (a "one-stop shop" for all things). So let's break down some of the reasons why productization is so beneficial for your business.

Clearly defined value to your target clients

Productizing services have a clearly defined scope of work and target outcome. Clients can easily understand what they will receive and the value they can expect as a result of working with you. This makes it easier to attract and close deals, and dramatically speeds up sales cycles.

Simplified sales processes

With standardized service packages, the sales process becomes more straightforward and efficient. Instead of customizing proposals for each client, the agency can present pre-defined offerings, reducing negotiation time and accelerating the sales cycle.

Scalability and operational efficiency

Productized services are designed to be repeatable and scalable. By streamlining and automating processes, the agency can handle multiple clients and projects simultaneously without sacrificing quality, leading to improved efficiency and resource management.

Consistency of work quality and results

When you do the same thing over and over again, all of your clients receive a consistent level of service and quality. This consistency results in fewer client complaints and better overall results. It also allows you to pinpoint errors in your process and make improvements quickly.

Predictably and consistently in your business

With standardized pricing and sales close rates, you can easily forecast revenue and growth. You know exactly how many leads it will take each month to meet your revenue goals, making your business more predictable for financial planning, budgeting and acquisition as well.

Upsells, downsells and cross-sells

Once a client has experienced the value of one service package, it becomes easier to upsell or cross-sell additional offerings. Satisfied clients are more likely to explore other standardized services that you provide.

Higher profit margins (by far)

When you do the same things over and over again, you need fewer people and software. You also don't need people with expensive skill sets, as it's far easier to train new staff members using the processes you have laid out. Our agency's net profits went from ~25% to ~60% after we fully productized.

Path to true automation

Everyone wants to automate their business, but you can't automate something that isn't standardized. We've been able to seamlessly integrate AI tools into our agency because everything is clearly defined. Without it, automation is impossible.

Competitive advantage in the market

In a crowded marketplace, productized services can provide a competitive advantage. Your well-defined offerings and efficient delivery can set you apart from competitors, attracting more clients and referrals. It also helps to position your agency as true experts, as you're viewed as solving a singular, painful problem. Most agencies are viewed as a jack of all trades, but a master of none. Productized agencies have a much clearer path to be viewed as true experts.

The biggest knock I get is something like this...

"My clients love us because we can handle everything for them. Design, SEO, email…we're a 1 stop shop".

Productizing your services doesn't stop you from that. What it stops you from is taking on random work that you've never done before, has unproven results and creates operational traffic jams inside your business.

Think of it like a restaurant menu. If a diner could walk into a restaurant and request any dish they imagine, the kitchen would be in chaos. But a menu, a select list of dishes the kitchen specializes in, ensures quality and efficiency. That's what productizing does for your agency.

I recall a number of times when, in the early stages of my first agency, we would take on website design projects (even though that was outside our normal scope of work) just because the client requested it, and we felt like we couldn't say no.

We would always justify it by saying "it's free money, we can't turn it down right now. Let's just do it, we will figure it out". The result was always the same. Weeks of confusion, delays, late nights, long weekends and a final product that wasn't up to our standards.

It taught us the importance of sticking to your systems. Anytime you break your systems, you are creating a ton of new work for yourself and your team. More work means worse results, and less profits.

How to Productize Your Service Offering

Now that I've sold you on the "why", let's talk about the "how".

Elements of a Productized Service

Every offer will differ, but generally speaking, there are elements that you should consider including in order to create a fully productized service offering.

1. **Singular audience type**. Obviously, we dedicated an entire chapter to this, you can't productize without a specific target market that the service caters to.

2. **Process standardization**. Defining a clear and consistent set of features, deliverables, and processes for the service. That means NO custom work or scope changes, your service is what it is.

3. **Clear, standard pricing**. Fixed price packages or subscription plans make it easy for customers to understand the costs.

4. **Clear scope of work/deliverables**. The client should know exactly what they will receive when they receive it, how much it costs and what they can expect as an end result.

5. **Pre-defined KPIs and reporting objectives**. Transparent performance metrics and regular reports to showcase the impact of your service offering.

Now let's talk about how you can get started productizing any service.

Step 1 - Map your offer

Delivering productized services starts with a high-level mind map of what you do, and how to deliver it.

Think of it like an assembly line in a factory, or a fast food joint, like McDonald's.

McDonald's Assembly Line

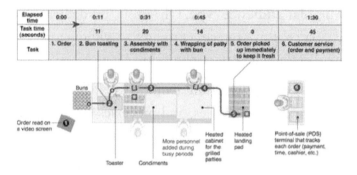

You can start with each of the pillars we created when designing your offer (remember, the roadblocks). I like to do this using a mind mapping tool, but you can also use old-fashioned pen and paper.

WEBRIS

- *Optimize local presence (review outreach, GBP, citations)*
- *Create key website content to rank for bottom-funnel search queries*
- *Acquire links via outreach to build authority and ranking equity*
- *Refocus PPC ads on long-tail keywords*

Now it's time to flush out each of these - what does it take to deliver on these? What are the individual actions/deliverables needed?

WEBRIS

- *Optimize local presence*

- *Optimize Google Business Profile*
  - *Add images and video*
  - *Setup review outreach campaign*
  - *Respond to existing reviews*
  - *Setup Q&A for highly asked questions*
- *Build local citations*
- *Optimize Avvo, FindLaw and Justia profiles*
- *Reach out to local newspapers for attorney profile features*
- *Create key website content to rank for bottom-funnel search queries*
  - *Create/optimize practice area pages*
  - *Create/optimize location pages*
  - *Optimize home page*
  - *Optimize page titles across the site*
  - *Setup internal linking silos across the site*
- *Acquire links via outreach to build authority and ranking equity*
  - *Build a list of relevant legal and local websites*
  - *Reach out to sites already inside our database*
  - *Reach out to relevant legal and local websites for link inclusions*
- *Refocus PPC ads on long-tail keywords*
  - *Audit past keyword and campaign performance*
  - *Research long-tail keywords*

- *Create new landing pages for mobile click-to-call*
- *Setup new ads (locally focused placements)*
- *Setup campaign performance reports*

This is your opportunity to go nuts on details. Flush out as much as you can think of, be exhaustive with this list. Soon you'll have a tree with branches, outlining every component of your core services.

Remember: keep your client in mind when mapping your offer. Think about their journey, their pain points, and how your service fits into their larger business goals.

But don't over complicate or over think anything at this stage. You just need to get everything out of your head and down on paper.

When that's done, move on to simplifying and standardizing service offerings, and creating processes.

Step 2 - Design your processes

A mind map is a necessary first step to flush out your service offering, but we're not done.

With a completed mind map you should clearly see everything that goes into delivering your service offering. Now we need to *strip it down* to focus on the key elements that will drive the **most impact**.

I like to do this by building a process flow. It takes all the elements from the mind map but turns it into an orderly process that can be followed/delivered as a service. The goal is to identify the items that deliver the most return while removing the vanity ones that do not drive towards the client's goal.

Each item in your mind map needs to be scrutinized.

- What is the point of this item?
- What people/software/skills are needed to deliver this?
- Is this [service/deliverable X] driving towards the main goal for our client?
- If we remove it, will it impact the end goal?

You might find there are deliverables that you either don't need or could be built out as stand-alone offerings. Dump anything that doesn't make sense or add value. Simplify and standardize the whole end-to-end process.

It's critically important that when stripping this down you stay focused on solving the macro problem for your target client.

Clients can see value more clearly when problems they've had for a while are being solved. It's also easier to start charging more when the impact value of your services increases.

With a completed process flow, you now have the foundational elements of a productized service. You have your service offered laid out in a way that shows all the items needed to take the client from start to finish.

Consider Amazon. Their order processing is impeccable, from the moment you click 'Buy Now' to the package arriving at your doorstep. This didn't happen by chance. It's the result of a meticulously designed process.

Now, it's time to turn it into a project plan template that can be executed as a service.

Step 3 - Create a project plan

Project planning is a major headache for a lot of agencies because every time a new client comes on, they scramble to build something from scratch.

If you follow our system, it's a simple copy-and-paste job to get a new client kicked off. A clear, repeatable way to deliver services at scale, over and over again.

Remember, keep it simple. Don't overcomplicate it. Don't be tempted to jam in a ton of deliverables to "fill it out". The only thing that matters is results for clients in the fastest, most efficient way possible.

> *It's not about how much work you put in, it's about how much your clients will get out of it.*

Try not to think about project management in terms of software - a lot of you get caught up trying to find the right tool when the tool is irrelevant. You can use a spreadsheet or pen and paper, as long as you have the core elements of a project plan you're all set.

Here's how to build your project plan template:

1. In a spreadsheet, list out all of the items needed to deliver your service (list them out vertically)

2. In the column next to it, list the role/person responsible for completing that item

3. In the next column, list how long it will take to complete the item

D	E	F	G
Fed Equp			
Project	Deliverable	Task	Status
Fed Equp	GA + GSC review	Deep look into accounts to ensure tracking is properly setup	Scheduled
Fed Equp	Kickoff Call	Finalize initial call with client + team	Scheduled
Fed Equp	Website Quality Audit	Setup Website Quality Audit (WQA)	Scheduled
Fed Equp	Website Quality Audit	Review WQA for **Technical** Action Items	Scheduled
Fed Equp	Website Quality Audit	Review WQA for **Content** Action Items	Scheduled
Fed Equp	Competitor KW Analysis	Document universe of keyword opportunities	Scheduled
Fed Equp	Content Workbook	Migrate URLs that will be worked on throughout the campaign	Scheduled
Fed Equp	SEO Strategy	Compile SEO strategy deck, send to client	Scheduled
Fed Equp	Strategy Call	Review SEO strategy deck with client, UPSELL!	Scheduled
Fed Equp	Sprint Report	Add additional lines to Project Plan	Scheduled
Fed Equp	Content Workbook	Compile topics, send to client for review	Scheduled
Fed Equp	Content Briefs	Create XX Content Briefs, send to client	Scheduled
Fed Equp	Sprint Report	Send report, UPSELL!	Scheduled
Fed Equp	Link Audit	Review link profile, gather findings, send to client for approval	Scheduled
Fed Equp	Link Acquisition	Secure XX links, add to report	Scheduled

That's it - that's the foundation of a project plan. Once you have the foundation, you can start to add more complexities on top of it, but the goal is to keep it simple. You really just need a bird's eye view of each client - *what do we need to do, who is going to do it, when will it be completed.*

If you are just getting started, use Google Sheets for project management. It's simple, effective and free. When a new client signs, make a copy of your template, assign roles + due dates and you're good to do.

As you scale you can move to an enterprise system that will allow you to load balance resources, track across multiple offers (i.e. PPC and SEO) and create Gantt timelines.

Our agency grew to over $1m in revenue using a simple Google Sheets project management system. We managed over 50 clients, each with unique requirements, yet our simple system kept us organized and on track. It's proof that you don't always need complex tools to scale; sometimes, simplicity is the key.

> **Head to theagencyblueprintbook.com to grab our FREE simple Google Sheets project management system for agencies.**

Step 4 - Create SOPs

We're almost done - the last step is to create Standard Operating Procedures (SOPs) to make this process scalable, repeatable and easy to train.

I'm not going to lie - SOPs are a lot of work. But it's the final step to pulling yourself out of operations. I suggest going to a cafe on a rainy Sunday so you can hammer these out with no distractions.

Ideally, every element of your business should be in an SOP - onboarding, service delivery, sales, etc. But by far the most important is service delivery.

I really want to stress that you don't need to overcomplicate an SOP. It is really just a documented set of step-by-step instructions that outline how to perform specific tasks or processes within your business.

There's no special template or format, you just need to dedicate the energy to documenting your service. Here's a few elements that you should include in your SOPs.

1. **Break down processes:** For each item, break down the processes involved into step-by-step instructions. Include details on how to initiate, execute, and complete each task.

2. **Document step-by-step instructions:** Write clear and detailed instructions for each step. Use bullet points or numbered lists for easy readability.

3. **Include best practices:** Incorporate best practices and tips to ensure the services are delivered efficiently and effectively.

4. **Consider different scenarios:** Anticipate potential challenges or variations that might arise during service delivery. Outline how to handle these situations.

5. **Add visuals:** Include relevant images, diagrams, or flowcharts to clarify complex processes or tasks. I also like to include screenshare videos giving an over-the-shoulder look at how to complete each item.

6. **Links and logins to necessary websites:** Make sure the person using the SOP has everything they need inside that document to do their job.

7. **Links to necessary internal templates**: Templates will be a big part of your processes, make sure to link to them as needed and also create the necessary training on how to use the templates.

Content Marketing Process

Table of Contents

- **Part 1: Building audience personas for content marketing**
  - ○ Check Google Analytics demographic reporting
  - ○ Check Facebook Audience Insights
  - ○ Check social media (Instagram, YouTube, Podcasts)
  - ○ Check customer data (ask client if you need to)
  - ○ Build 1 - 3 audience personas into template

- **Part 2: Generating topics for content creation**
  - ○ Using internal site search reporting in Google Analytics
  - ○ Niche up from "bottom of funnel" keywords
  - ○ Use keyword gap analysis document
  - ○ Steal from competitors using SEM Rush
  - ○ Upgrade past topics using SEM Rush

- **Part 3: Vetting topics and completing the workbook**
  - ○ Checking for keywords and volume using Google Suggest + Keywords everywhere
  - ○ Using the MozBar to flush out competition
  - ○ Selecting keywords and recording them
  - ○ Assigning the stage in the journey
  - ○ Picking the right type of content for the topic
  - ○ Adding detailed notes for the content manager to build outlines

SOPs are integral to the internal training process. At WEBRIS, we have 30, 60 and 90-day training sprints. At the end of these training cycles, we expect new team members to take ownership of the SOP. This way, they can train and lead new hires once time tracking shows they are approaching capacity.

I remember a new hire, Adam. Initially, he felt overwhelmed. But with our 30-day training sprint, guided by our SOPs, he quickly became one of our top performers. By his 90-day mark, he was training other new members. This is the power of structured, comprehensive SOPs.

SOPs give staff a solid framework. Give them the tools they need to do the work. Empower and encourage them; trust them to execute and deliver. Guide them when mistakes are made, and watch your agency scale while your input gradually reduces.

Over time, revisit and refine these templates based on feedback and evolving business needs. This iterative process ensures your templates remain current and effective.

And there we go. That's the steps you need to take to transform a custom service-based agency into a scalable, productized SEO agency.

Taking the journey from a traditional agency model to a productized one isn't an overnight endeavor. Yet, the rewards are immense. As you proceed, remember to be agile. Refine your processes based on experience, feedback, and evolving business needs. Picture a future where your agency operations are streamlined, clients are consistently satisfied, and your involvement is strategic rather than day-to-day. That future is attainable, and these exercises are the first steps in that direction.

Action Steps for Mastering Offer Productization

Now that we've explored the significance and process of Offer Productization, it's time to put theory into practice. These exercises are designed to guide you in taking tangible steps toward productizing your services.

1. The "Why"

Contemplate your reasons for wanting to productize your services.

- *Note down three past challenges faced due to a lack of productization.*

- *What potential benefits of productization resonate with you the most? List them.*

- *Visualize how your agency will operate once services are productized.*

2. Mind Mapping

Use a tool or plain paper to mind map your current services.

- *List down the key services you offer.*

- *For each service, detail the sub-tasks or deliverables involved.*

- *Identify any gaps or redundancies.*

3. Process Flow

Transform your mind map into a streamlined process flow.

- *Review each item in your mind map: Does it directly contribute to client goals?*

- *Eliminate or modify non-essential items.*

- *Arrange the remaining items in a logical, efficient sequence.*

4. Project Plan

Design a simple project plan template for your productized service.

- *Using a spreadsheet, list all tasks or deliverables vertically.*

- *Assign roles or personnel responsible for each task.*

- *Estimate the duration for each task.*

5. Standard Operating Procedure (SOP)

Document the detailed steps for executing each service.

- *For each task or deliverable, write step-by-step instructions.*

- *Integrate best practices and common challenges.*

- *Add visuals, templates, and links as needed for clarity.*

Head to theagencyblueprintbook.com to claim your FREE workbooks from this chapter.

PILLAR 3

Service Mastery

The foundation of your business is now set. You've built an offer that your target client can't refuse, and you've turned it into a scalable system.

If pillars one and two are about setting the stage, pillar three is the performance itself. Here's where the magic happens, where you prove your worth, and where you build client relationships that last a lifetime.

Nailing these first two pillars will ensure your ability to always make money. But if you want to become a business, with long-term staying power and market equity, you need to become a master of your domain.

That means becoming a true master of your service offering and understanding your client's business at a deeper level.

At WEBRIS, we service law firms - it's arguably one of the most competitive spaces for an agency to operate. There's a ton of agency competition who are all incredibly adept at marketing and acquisition.

Most law firms don't know that much about marketing - so when we tried to differentiate ourselves based on our search marketing skills, they didn't care. Our pitches about the quality of our services didn't land.

But when we started immersing ourselves in their world, we saw a massive shift in sales close rates. Instead of just learning about marketing and SEO, we started learning about the legal process, the law firm business model and the challenges they face on a daily basis.

We quickly saw a huge increase in sales and realized that understanding the client's world on a deeper level was the key to success. That's why we always take the time to understand our clients inside out before pitching any campaigns or services. We develop an intimate knowledge of their industry, their competition, and their customers so we can tailor our approach accordingly and maximize the impact of our services.

Let's look at the story of a Los Angeles based marketing agency that was struggling to make an impact in the crowded e-commerce marketing space. They had the skills, the team, and the passion, but they were just another agency in a sea of many. They decided to shift their focus from just selling marketing services to understanding the e-commerce business inside out.

They started attending e-commerce conventions, partnering with e-commerce platforms, and even set up their own dummy e-commerce store to test out strategies. In six months, they had gathered a plethora of real-world data and experiences which they used to revamp their service offerings. Their pitches to potential clients now included real data, real challenges, and real solutions. The result? A 200% increase in client acquisition in the next year.

The takeaway? You need to become obsessed with solving your customers' problems. Not just their marketing and acquisition problems, but their existential business problems as well.

If you can turn yourself into a master of your client's business, not just a master of acquisition, you become immortal.

I tell people all the time - our agency offers search marketing services to law firms because it is the best way to get them leads right now. While we know search marketing inside and out, we don't exist to do search marketing - we exist to solve problems for law firms.

If (and when) Google blows up, we'll be ready. We'll just move to the next best acquisition strategy in line. In fact, I secretly hope Google dies out because we'll take over the market.

How to become a master of your client's domain

Imagine you're at a party, and someone is talking about a recent vacation they took to Italy. If you've never been to Italy or studied it, you might nod along, but if you've lived in Italy for a year, your engagement level in that conversation is entirely different. You can discuss the food, the local spots, the culture, and share personal anecdotes. The depth of your engagement is much richer. That's the difference between just offering a service and mastering your client's domain.

This will be the shortest chapter, as each of you reading this will have your own unique offer. Since there are nuances in what you do vs what we do, I can't teach you exactly how to master your client's domain in this book.

No two industries are the same. The nuances, the challenges, the customers - everything varies. And therein lies the magic potion for your agency's success: understanding these unique elements.

Service mastery is a core focus inside of The Blueprint Training, as we're able to work 1 on 1 with you to help you understand what the best strategies available to you are right now.

But for now, I can give you the process I follow to master skill sets.

The mastery process

Bruce Lee once said, 'I fear not the man who has practiced 10,000 kicks once, but I fear the man who has practiced one kick 10,000 times.' Mastery is about depth, not width.

There are really two things you need to focus on when mastering anything:

1. **Committing to learning**. Immerse yourself in their world, commit to becoming the best in the world at what you do. That starts with believing you are the best and speaking it into existence. You are an F badass, don't let anyone tell you differently.

2. **Patience and time**. There's no speeding this up, it's a marathon, not a sprint. You can't learn everything overnight, all you can do is put 1 foot in front of the other and start walking up that hill.

Energy goes where the intention flows. When you are intentional about doing something, good things happen. Commit to daily action, here are a few tips on how:

1. Get active on social media

X (Twitter), Facebook, LinkedIn, Instagram, TikTok, or whatever social network is popping off when you're reading this book. They're all goldmines for learning because they allow you to join the conversation.

Start with a content calendar. Dedicate Mondays to sharing industry news, Wednesdays for interactive polls or quizzes, and Fridays for a sneak peek into your agency's life. Engage with comments, share client success stories, and participate in relevant hashtag trends.

I have an X "List" that aggregates thought leaders, legal publications and competitors in the space. I check it every other day to catch up on legal news, headlines and information that's pertinent to my daily work.

Don't just consume, create. Create a new profile if you want that is purely business and learning-focused. Get active in threads, debate with people, and force yourself to think.

2. Document the nuances over time

Create a digital repository, using tools like Notion or Evernote, where you categorize and store these nuances. Regularly review and update this database. Over time, this will become your goldmine for crafting tailor-made strategies for clients.

SEO for lawyers is different from SEO for an ecommerce store. There are nuances in our service offering that we continue to discover the further we go down this path of mastery. I have a running list of nuanced strategies that I keep in a notes file that I use to refine our service and create marketing material. Here's a copy and pasted section from my notes as an example:

When searching for a law firm's website in Google, most of the websites ranking are aggregator websites like FindLaw, Justia and Avvo. We need to figure out a way to get our clients active on these websites, because they are a gold mine for organic referrals. We should also look into advertising on these platforms as an upsell offer.

3. Do it for yourself

Whenever we launch a new service offering, we do it for ourselves first. Not only do we want to make sure the results are there, but we want to flush out all parts of the process and make sure everyone internally is well versed in it.

There's a depth of understanding that comes from doing things firsthand. It's the difference between reading about swimming and actually diving into the pool.

If you want to learn how to do SEO for a law firm website, build your own law firm website and figure it out. If you want to learn how to generate sales for an ecommerce store using TikTok ads, set up your own store and do it yourself.

I know it's a lot of work, but it's the best way to learn, by far. Plus, you'll have a case study that you can use to attract new clients that you own outright.

4. Create your own templates

While generic templates provide a foundation, customized templates resonate more. They show clients that you're not just offering a one-size-fits-all solution but crafting a strategy specifically for them.

Inside of The Blueprint Training, we give our clients a full suite of done-for-you service delivery templates. However, we encourage our clients to make them their own. There's something incredibly powerful about rethinking how to do things specifically for your clients, with your offer.

5. Attend live events and networking opportunities

Not just marketing conferences, go to events that are built for your target client. A simple Google search for "[target industry] conferences" will turn up a ton of information to get you started.

Attending industry-specific events not only provides learning opportunities but also places you right in the midst of potential clients. It gives you a chance to understand their pain points firsthand, engage in real-time discussions, and even showcase some of your success stories.

6. Research and try tools

I don't mean tools that you can use to deliver your service, I mean tools that would potentially help your client in other areas. Before a client comes to you with a problem, be the agency that identifies it and offers a solution. Maybe it's a new CRM tool or an AI-driven analytics platform. Your proactive approach will not only solve their issues but position you as an indispensable partner in their growth.

For example, I've learned that law firms struggle with sales operations. They rarely use a CRM or any sort of technology to help themselves out. While we don't offer sales services, I've done the research on helpful sales tools that can help them out.

This is impactful for a number of reasons:

1. It builds trust with the client, because I am helping them out and not charging them.

2. The client views us as a trusted source of information that can be given more work over time.

3. It helps us extend the life of our contracts. We can drive leads all day to law firms, but if they can't close them we're useless.

7. Follow industry leaders closely

For instance, if you're in the SEO world, following leaders like Rand Fishkin or Neil Patel can provide invaluable insights. They often share cutting-edge strategies, algorithm updates, and tools that can elevate your service delivery.

Read their case studies, watch their webinars, and analyze their strategies. Not only will you learn a great deal from this type of research, but it could also help to bring in new clients.

8. Network in the Industry

Networking isn't just about adding connections on LinkedIn. Join digital marketing forums, communities, and LinkedIn groups. Engage in meaningful conversations, collaborate on joint ventures, or even consider setting up monthly virtual meetups with fellow professionals. These interactions often lead to shared learnings and potential referrals.

9. Teach others through content creation

Share your knowledge through blog posts, tutorials, or workshops. It does two things: it positions you as an expert in your field and helps you understand your domain even better. Consider hosting webinars, crafting detailed case studies, or even running short online courses.

10. Continue to invest in yourself

Never stop learning and experimenting with new SEO tactics. The digital marketing field evolves rapidly, and staying ahead requires ongoing education.

Set aside a dedicated 'learning hour' every week. This could be for online courses, reading industry reports, or even brainstorming innovative strategies. The world of digital marketing evolves rapidly. Stay ahead by being a lifelong learner.

In conclusion, service mastery isn't just about being good at what you do; it's about being the best while continuously adapting and growing. It's a journey, not a destination. As you delve deeper into this world, remember to keep your clients at the heart of everything. Their success is your success. Now, gear up as we dive into the next pillar, where we discuss how to amplify your reach and build a brand that resonates.

A huge part of what we do for our agency clients at The Blueprint Training is help you stay ahead of the curve when it comes to your service. We work with you to ensure you are always "in the know" about the best strategies to get your clients results. Head to theblueprint.training to learn more.

Action Steps for Achieving Service Mastery

This chapter delved deep into the importance of mastering your services and truly understanding your client's domain. As we step off the stage of setting the foundation and now focus on the performance, here are actionable exercises to help you embody the principles of Service Mastery.

1. Industry Immersion

The best way to understand an industry is to immerse yourself in it.

- *List down 3 leading conferences or events in your client's domain that you can attend.*

- *Name 5 thought leaders in your client's domain. Begin following them on social media and set a monthly reminder to check on any new insights they've shared.*

- *Find 3 online forums or communities specific to your client's domain. Engage in them weekly.*

2. Deep Dive into Your Client's World

Go beyond the surface to understand the intricacies of your client's business.

- *Identify a client (or a potential one). Research and list down the top 5 challenges their industry is currently facing.*

- *Draft a brief strategy or solution you could offer to mitigate one of these challenges.*

- *Conduct a SWOT analysis (Strengths, Weaknesses, Opportunities, Threats) for this client.*

3. Tools and Resources

Stay ahead by understanding the tools that can aid your client's business.

- *Research and list down 3 tools or platforms that could potentially help your client in areas outside of your primary services.*

- *Document how each tool could benefit your client.*

- *Consider reaching out to these tool providers. Can you form a partnership or gain insights that can further help your clients?*

4. Content Mastery Challenge

Position yourself as an expert by sharing knowledge.

- *Draft an outline for a blog post or article, sharing insights about a recent trend in your client's industry.*

- *Plan a webinar or a workshop where you can teach a relevant skill or strategy to your clients.*

- *Identify 3 platforms or forums where you can share this content and engage with potential clients or industry professionals.*

5. Continuous Learning Plan

Map out your journey of continuous learning.

- *List down 3 online courses or certifications that can enhance your skills or knowledge about your client's domain.*

- *Set a recurring weekly 'learning hour' in your calendar. Use this time to read industry reports, new research, or explore innovative strategies.*

- *Consider creating a 'knowledge repository'. A digital space (like Notion, Evernote) where you store insights, strategies, and observations about your client's industry.*

PILLAR 4

Client Acquisition

Finally, here's the part most of you have been itching to get to. I've got a hunch some of you might've even jumped ahead to this section.

How do I know that?

Last year we ran a survey of the 3,000 agencies we've worked with, asking them what they believed to be the number 1 thing holding them back from meeting their goals.

Over 80% responded "lack of leads" as their number one problem.

But, spoiler alert: it's not always about generating leads. If you're unsure about who you're trying to attract or your offer is as bland as unsalted popcorn, you're setting yourself up for a lead drought. And let's not even start with offering a subpar service. So if you've been snoozing during Pillars 1, 2, and 3, I'd suggest a quick recap.

However, for those who've been paying attention, it's showtime. Let's dive into making sure your offer doesn't just sit pretty but gets the eyeballs it deserves.

Lead generation 101

Of all the chapters in this book, this one is by far the most difficult to write.

Most of you are probably reading this expecting to see information on marketing channels—how to generate leads through LinkedIn, outbound DMs, content marketing, and whatnot. But here's what I want this book to be: timeless. I want the concepts and strategies I lay out here to still apply in 2030, 2040, and beyond.

See, the thing with marketing channels is that they come and go. If you're reading this five years down the line, chances are the channels I recommend today won't be as effective anymore. I've seen dozens of marketing tactics come and go in my career. **The businesses that succeed are not the ones who understand tactics, but the ones that understand people.**

Marketing channels like Instagram, Google, and YouTube are just communication platforms. They evolve and adapt based on how humans prefer to consume content. If you want to generate leads successfully, it's simply a matter of building communication channels that are focused on addressing your client's problems.

We've spent the first 3 chapters of this book discussing how you can find problems for a specific type of client and build solutions that generate results. Now it's time to scream from the top of rooftops that's what you do.

Speak to me like I'm 5

Your job is to talk about your client's problems and how to solve them. It's really that simple. A lot of you are hung up on which channel to use, yet I guarantee if I look at your social media profiles you haven't posted a single time about your business. How can you expect to get leads, if you don't actively promote your offer?

I get it, you're paralyzed by overthinking the process. What if someone reads it and doesn't like what you have to say? What if no one engages with your post? Well, those are risks you have to take if you want to generate leads.

You don't need to be Gary Vaynerchuck. What you need is a clear message that resonates with your target audience's core problems and offers solutions. To achieve this, you need:

- **Messaging** - You want your potential clients to instantly get what you're offering and why it matters to them. It's not about you; it's about them and their problems. And most importantly, you're the solution they've been searching for. Remember: this is not about using fancy business jargon. It's about clear, direct communication that speaks their language.

  Example: If you offer social media marketing services, don't talk about what you do "We do social media" focus on your target client's headaches/problems "Most law firms struggle generating leads, here's 3 things you need to do on LinkedIn to get more cases".

- **Attention** - You can't sell something if you don't have your audience's attention. You need to be present in the places that your target clients are hanging out. If they're scrolling through LinkedIn during their lunch breaks, that's your cue. Dive into the platforms, forums, and spaces they hang out in. Engage with them genuinely, understanding their likes and dislikes.

  Example: If your potential clients are struggling to understand how AI will impact their business, consider hosting a webinar on embracing AI. Share it on the platforms they use, and promote it to your audience.

- **Consistency** - This is where many people drop the ball. One-off messages are just that - here today, gone tomorrow. But when you consistently show up, offering value, insights, or solutions? That's how you stay top of mind. It's the repeated rhythms that build trust and familiarity, creating lasting connections. Never ghost your following, even if it seems small and you don't get a lot of traction. Rome wasn't built in a day.

  Example: Keep your blog up-to-date and regularly share on social media. If you start a series with best tips for limited time product campaigns, finish it before moving onto the next thing.

Lead generation is all about delivering value. At the end of every click, every view, every engagement, there's a person struggling with headaches, problems, fears and anxieties. And if you can genuinely connect with that person, I assure you, you've already won half the battle.

Now that we've covered the basics, let's talk about putting this into action. In order to generate leads with marketing that nails messaging, grabs attention and is consistent, we need a mechanism to do so.

That's where content comes into play, it's the engine that makes all marketing campaigns go.

Why content is *actually* king

The phrase "Content is King" is thrown around often, but rarely executed properly. The internet is filled with bad content - content that was created for the sake of content.

"Content" isn't about creating a hundred blog posts or videos, it's the best vehicle to connect with potential clients and position yourself as an authority. You do this through creating the right type of content, with the right cadence or volume).

Content is the most important marketing asset there is, for a number of reasons:

1. It allows you to lead with value (not commercials)
2. It allows you to educate / nurture your audience
3. It allows you to be hyper-present across channels
4. It allows you to leverage owned, earned and paid tactics

In many ways, content is the glue that holds your marketing campaigns together. It's an essential ingredient you simply can't do without. Content is the only mechanism that allows you to connect with your audience around their problems.

That said, context matters. To maximize impact, you need the right content type, tailored depth, and distribution strategy.

How to create content that resonates

> *"Content marketing is like a first date. If you only talk about yourself, there won't be a second one." - David Beebe, CEO at Storified*

When you're striving to build a connection with your audience, your content needs to be more than just words on a page or images on a screen. It has to reverberate with the needs, desires, and pain points of your target clients.

To determine what will truly strike a chord, you need to develop a **thesis**. Think of it as your content's north star—a clear, concise point of view that allows you to create content that both engages prospects *and* draws them into your funnel.

At its core, a marketing thesis defines:

1. **Your Brand's Stance:** It solidifies your brand's viewpoint on your customer's core problems, fears and anxieties.

2. **The Value Proposition:** It should clearly outline why your audience should care. What makes your perspective unique or beneficial to them?

3. **Competitor Differentiation**: A thesis can help you set yourself apart from competitors by highlighting your brand's unique benefits and why customers should choose you over them.

Developing a thesis for your brand is a complex strategy, so let's look at some examples to try and drill this home.

Let's circle back to WEBRIS and our "blended search approach". Now, if we follow the instructions we just discussed, we end up with a marketing thesis that looks a little something like this:

Your Brand's Stance:

> *"The legal industry is arguably one of the most competitive on the planet. There's more law firms than ever spending a ton of*

money on digital channels. This has dramatically increased the cost to enter the market and get results. Most marketing strategies do not work anymore because of this. Ads are too expensive because CPMs are so high you can't get profitable. Billboards and radio ads are a waste of your money because no one sees them. Social media is a waste of time because it takes too much energy to create daily content, and no one really uses social media to find a lawyer anyways. But search marketing is a perfect fit - prospects are actively searching for you right now in your local market, you just have to be present. However, most law firms know this, so they are spending a lot of money there, making it brutally competitive. In order to be successful in search engines, lawyers need to adapt their strategy to focus on multiple facets of search (LSAs, PPC, maps pack, traditional listings)"

The Value Proposition:

"By adopting a 'blended' search strategy, law firms combine the immediacy of Pay-Per-Click (PPC) ads with the long-term benefits of organic rankings. In addition, this strategy attacks all parts of search results - local maps pack, traditionail organic listings, PPC ads, and local service ads. This ensures consistent visibility across search engine results, catering to the diverse search habits of potential clients. More than just visibility, this approach is about delivering tangible value, building trust, and ensuring that every potential client interaction is meaningful and impactful."

Competitor Differentiation:

> *"Most law firms have tried SEO or PPC before and failed. That's because most agencies don't understand how to execute a multi faceted search approach. By targeting both paid and organic opportunities, we offer a unique and comprehensive solution, ensuring that our clients stand out in a saturated market and are always a step ahead of their competitors."*

One more thing to mention, a good marketing thesis should be relevant for 12-24 months. It's not just some passing idea, but rather a long-term commitment to a specific message or concept. You'll want to apply it consistently across your social media, email campaigns, paid ads, and all other forms of marketing, both online and offline. This way, you dramatically boost your chances of success.

Finally, keep in mind that your thesis statement should be revisited and adjusted as needed to ensure it remains focused and relevant to the ever-changing industry landscape. It needs to remain flexible enough to capture the true essence of your brand no matter the channel or medium.

Why is it crucial? Without a defined marketing thesis:

- You run the risk of talking about things that have no relation to your service. In other words, content for the sake of content, instead of content for the sake of leads.

- You lose out on establishing your brand as a thought leader in your niche. A consistent and well-defined message helps in building authority and niche relevancy.

- It becomes challenging to measure the effectiveness of your content. With a set thesis, you have a benchmark to evaluate your content against.

Integrating the Marketing Thesis into Content Creation

Once you have your marketing thesis in place, every piece of content you produce should echo its sentiments. Here's how you can ensure that:

1. **Audience Persona:** Always keep your target audience in mind. Understand their challenges, motivations, and desires. Your marketing thesis should address these aspects.

2. **Consistent Messaging:** Whether it's a blog post, a social media update, or a podcast episode, ensure that the content aligns with your marketing thesis.

3. **Feedback Loop:** Regularly collect feedback on your content. Are your readers finding value? Is it resonating with them? Use this feedback to fine-tune your content strategy.

4. **Content Formats:** Not everyone consumes content in the same way. While your marketing thesis remains consistent, adapt its presentation based on the platform. For instance, an infographic might work better on Instagram, while a detailed article might be more suited for your blog.

In essence, your marketing thesis serves as the anchor, ensuring that your content not only resonates but also drives home the message you want to convey. It's the difference between merely producing content and crafting content that strikes a chord.

Leveraging tested content frameworks

With your thesis in hand, it's time to start flushing out things to talk about. The most important thing to keep in mind is this isn't about "you" and what you offer, it's about your clients.

The key to creating content that resonates is focusing on your client's problems. The reason is simple - people are mainly concerned with themselves. If you find yourself creating content that's all about "you", no one will care.

Every piece of content you create needs to be about "them", the best way to do that is talking about the problems they face on a daily basis (as it relates to your thesis). I like to create a mindmap of my client's problems, then insert those problems into the frameworks above.

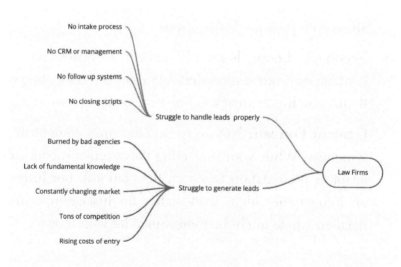

The image above is an example of a law firm's problems, as they relate to our offer and thesis. The key is to flush out some core problems, then continuously expand on them. Each of those sub problems allows me to create 10 to 15 pieces of content addressing them. This is how you ensure that you never run out of things to say and that you always stay within your thesis.

Flush out as many sub topics as you can (more than 100). Once you have those, you can leverage content creation frameworks to turn those ideas into pieces of content. Creating content can be incredibly challenging, most people don't know where to begin. You don't have to reinvent the wheel, you can frameworks that will allow you to always create content that resonates with your audience and maps to your thesis.

I like to transfer topics into a Content Workbook to stay organized. In the workbook I'll jot down the topic, type of content and notes that flush out the topic into a full piece of content. This allows me to stay organized and consistent with my content creation.

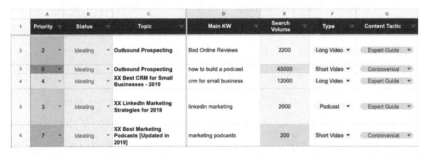

	Priority	Status	Topic	Main KW	Search Volume	Type	Content Tactic
1							
2	2	Ideating	Outbound Prospecting	Bad Online Reviews	2200	Long Video	Expert Guide
3	9	Ideating	Outbound Prospecting	how to build a podcast	45000	Short Video	Controversial
4	4	Ideating	XX Best CRM for Small Businesses - 2019	crm for small business	12000	Long Video	Expert Guide
5	3	Ideating	XX LinkedIn Marketing Strategies for 2019	linkedin marketing	2000	Podcast	Expert Guide
6	7	Ideating	XX Best Marketing Podcasts [Updated in 2019]	marketing podcasts	200	Short Video	Controversial

The Content Workbook is included in the free template suite you can grab at theagencyblueprintbook.com.

Now let's talk about putting pen to paper and turning these topics into pieces of content.

PAS Framework - Problem, Agitation, Solution

Copywriting frameworks ensure you are always nailing the problems your readers are facing, and provide them with a well-crafted solution. The PAS Framework is my personal go-to. It's like having a personal chat, where you truly understand their struggles and offer a compelling answer to their needs. It goes like this:

1. **State the Problem:** Begin by outlining the issue your audience grapples with. This lays the foundation for what's to come.

2. **Agitate:** After identifying the problem, amplify its significance. This isn't about fear-mongering; it's about underscoring the genuine need for a solution.

3. **Present the Solution:** Now, position your agency as the beacon of hope. Show them how you're uniquely positioned to resolve the challenges they face.

Example: *"Frustrated with spending countless hours on tax sorting? Want to avoid those hefty penalties that even a small mistake can cause? Our expert tax service has got your back. With us, you'll not only save time and money but also steer clear of those pesky fines."*

The Before and After Framework

This approach works similarly to the Problem/Solution framework, but it focuses more on appealing to the user's emotions and imagination, rather than their logic. It's all about describing the challenges they are facing and how those difficulties are limiting them from achieving success or happiness:

1. **Paint a picture of your readers' current reality**: Describe what your readers are going through day-to-day before they have access to your solution. Show how tedious and inefficient their current process is, and the state of dissatisfaction they feel when looking for an answer.

2. **Reveal the solution and describe their lives using it**: Explain how your product or service solves their problem, providing a better outcome and a more efficient way of doing things. Show them the light at the end of the tunnel and provide steps on how to get there.

Example: *"Currently, you're spending three hours every week trying to write a single blog post. With our content strategy guide, you'll be pumping out killer blog posts in just 30 minutes, saving you time to focus on growing your business."*

AIDA Framework - Attention, Interest, Desire, Action

The AIDA Framework is a tried-and-tested marketing technique that emphasizes engaging the user's attention, stirring up their interest and curiosity, building desire to learn more about the product or service, and then urging them to take action, typically by creating FOMO.

1. **Attention:** Commence with compelling headlines and hooks. Your primary goal? Grab their attention.

2. **Interest:** Once you have their attention, educate them about the issue. Elucidate its nuances and intricacies.

3. **Desire:** Build on the interest by showcasing how your agency can be their game-changer. Make them yearn for what you offer.

4. **Action:** Round it off with a call-to-action. Whether it's getting in touch, signing up, or making a purchase, guide them towards the next step.

Example: *"Are you tired of not getting enough leads despite all your efforts? Get ready to be amazed at how quickly your leads will pour in with our new content strategy guide. Our easy-to-follow blueprint will help you create blog posts that engage and convert more customers than ever before. Get it for free before 30th September!"*

By now, you should have a mind map listing out all of your client's biggest problems, and you should have a basic understanding of how you can begin to communicate those problems with frameworks. We're almost ready to start creating content - but first, we need to cover the various types at your disposal.

Understand the nuances of content "type"

Content comes in various forms - from short social posts to long-form guides, webinar videos to 15 second video clips, the options are endless. The type of content you create is generally dictated by the platform you publish on. For example, long form video (12 to 30 minutes) works best on YouTube, where short form video (30 to 60 seconds) performs best on TikTok or Instagram.

You need to understand the types of content that align with your skillset and where that performs best. It's the fine line between content that gets lost in the shuffle and content that captivates. Let's break down some of the primary content distinctions and how best to utilize them:

1. Long Form vs Short Form

- **Long Form**: These are your deep dives. Think of articles or videos that tackle a topic in-depth, e-books, or comprehensive guides. They're valuable for:
    - Establishing authority and expertise in a subject.
    - Offering readers a one-stop resource on a particular topic.
    - Improving organic search engine rankings, as search engines often favor detailed content.
    - *Example*: Imagine an agency crafting an extensive guide on "The Anatomy of Successful Meta Ads for Ecommerce Brands."
- **Short Form**: This is content that's quick to consume. Think of social media posts, brief blog updates, or short videos. They're ideal for:
    - Engaging with audiences who have shorter attention spans.
    - Offering quick tips, updates, or news.
    - Driving frequent engagement on social media.
    - *Example*: A 30 second video for YouTube shorts covering an email subject line that garnered a 70% open rate ("THIS Email Got A 70% Open Rate").

2. Video vs Written

- **Video**: With the rise of platforms like YouTube, TikTok, and Instagram, video content is more popular than ever. Video is potent for:

  - Demonstrating a product or process.

  - Building a much deeper audience connection, as viewers see, hear and *feel* you.

  - Engages people on the move or who want to consume content faster (2x speed).

  - *Example*: A digital agency discussing their process for a B2B SaaS website redesign on a Facebook Live video.

- **Written**: This classic form remains essential. Whether it's articles, e-books, or social media posts, written content is key for:

  - Deep dives into topics.

  - Reaching audiences who prefer reading over watching.

  - Providing detailed information that can be easily referenced.

  - Performs best organically in search engines for hands free traffic / growth.

  - *Example*: A case study showcasing how an outdated website was transformed into a conversion machine.

3. Paid vs Organic

- **Paid**: This refers to content promotion that you pay for, like ads. Paid content is beneficial for:

  - Achieving immediate visibility.

- Targeting specific demographics or audiences.

- Promoting time-sensitive offers or products.

- *Example*: A targeted ad campaign for an upcoming masterclass on "Decoding the Digital Consumer's Mind in 2023."

- **Organic**: This is content that naturally reaches audiences without direct payment, primarily through search engines or shares. Organic content shines in:

  - Building lasting brand credibility.

  - Engaging audiences without an advertising budget.

  - Achieving long-term visibility, especially if it ranks well on search engines.

  - *Example*: Consistent blog posts on a digital agency's site, diving into niche topics like "How to run marketing campaigns for law firms," slowly but steadily climbing the Google ranks.

To sum up: you've got plenty of options. Don't get overwhelmed, focus on a single type of content that works for you. If you can't write, use video. If you hate being on camera, focus on a podcast. If you can drill into a singular type of content you can consistently create, you've got what you need to start reaching your customers. Here's a quick recap of the content creation process.

1. Start by flushing out your target client's problems into a mind map. Exhaust all possibilities, the more you come up with the better, as these will serve as the topics you talk about.

2. Next, flush out those problems into topics inside of your Content Workbook.

3. Assign a content type (written, video, audio) that aligns with who you are and what you do best.

Stop making excuses for yourself - you're not going to be perfect when you get started. Running a business is hard, if it were easy, everyone would do it. Aim to test and tailor over time. Try a mix of short and long-form content, blend video and written formats. The more you experiment, the more you'll uncover what works best for you.

Crafting content that truly resonates is no walk in the park. But here's the kicker - after all that effort, you're only halfway there. Now, it's time to ensure that content reaches the right eyes and ears.

How to distribute content

Content distribution is a crucial aspect of any brand or company's marketing strategy. It helps to determine how many people will actually see your content. That's why it pays to understand the best ways to reach your target audience and get them engaged.

There are several channels that can be used for distribution:

1. Owned Channels

This is your home base. Every brand or company has platforms they own and control. These are assets where you decide the content, the look, and the frequency.

- **Examples**: Your website, your blog, newsletters, and your social media profiles.

- **Strength**: Total control. You decide the message, the design, and when and how it goes out.

- **How to start**: Get active! I'm willing to bet you don't post on social media everyday, write content for your blog, or create videos for YouTube. These are FREE marketing channels that need to be your priority. At the very least, you should be posting to LinkedIn once a day. Until you do that, you don't have the right to complain about a lack of leads.

2. Earned Channels

When your content is so good that others share, mention, or promote it without you paying them, that's earned content. It's like a word-of-mouth recommendation in the digital realm.

- **Examples**: Social media shares by fans or influencers, reviews, press mentions, and any content that goes 'viral'.

- **Strength**: Authenticity. When others promote your content, it often carries more weight because it comes across as a genuine endorsement.

- **How to start**: If you owned an ecommerce store, "earned" promotions would most likely come from influencers talking about your products. In the b2b agency space, it's mostly going to come from people who are engaging with your social media posts, which will in turn boost your visibility with social algorithms. You can't hit a home run if you don't take a swing, so the first thing you need to do is get active and start posting. Then, engage / comment on other people's posts to draw attention back to yours and support their content. Do this everyday for 90 days, your content will perform much better.

3. Paid Content

Sometimes, to ensure your content gets in front of the right eyes, you need to invest. This is where paid content distribution comes into play.

- **Examples**: Social media ads, Google Ads, sponsored articles, and display advertisements on relevant sites.

- **Strength**: Precision. You can target specific demographics, locations, or behaviors, ensuring your content reaches those most likely to engage.

- **How to start**: We'll talk about this more in a moment...

Organic vs. Paid: The Eternal Debate

It's a common discussion in marketing circles: which is better, organic or paid? But the reality is, you don't have to pick sides.

- **Organic** is foundational. By consistently producing and sharing valuable content on your owned channels, you build a reputation and draw in audiences over time. It's about establishing trust and credibility. Think of it as cultivating a garden; you plant seeds (content), water them (engage with your audience), and over time, you reap the benefits.

- **Paid** is strategic. When you want to target a specific group, launch a new product, or promote a limited-time offer, paid content can put your message directly in front of those who matter most. It's like setting up a spotlight; it ensures the right people see what you have to offer, right when you want them to see it.

Distributing content effectively is a balancing act. Rely solely on organic, and you miss short-term opportunities. Depend only on paid, and you lack long-term authority. The truth is, both organic and paid content have vital roles to play.

Start by building a solid content foundation on owned channels. Earn credibility and community organically over time. Then layer in paid distribution for precision targeting and immediate reach.

Evaluate performance and refine your strategy. Double down on what resonates best with your audience. With an orchestrated distribution plan, you amplify your message far beyond what any single channel could achieve.

Remember, distribution is about reaching the right people at the right time on the right platforms. Take an omnichannel approach, leverage paid and organic in harmony, and your content will thrive. Cutting through the noise is challenging, but a sound distribution plan delivers your message to eager ears.

What your agency should do, right now

Now that we covered the evergreen foundational elements of generating leads, let's talk about the specific tactics of what you should be doing right now. Our agency (WEBRIS) generates over 50 qualified leads per month, all of them inbound. You don't have to do a million things.

Here's the 3 activities I recommend, in order:

1. Post daily on LinkedIn

LinkedIn is a gold mine. Not only is it the only social network that's meant for businesses, but the LinkedIn algorithm favors creators. It's one of the last (if only) social networks that still rewards creators with a ton of organic (free) exposure.

A lot of you think you have to be on every platform...you don't. Every platform requires a different type of content to be successful there (think TikTok vs Twitter). It's far more effective to build a deep presence on a single social network, than spread yourself thin over 5.

So let me just save you the time - focus on LinkedIn!

The key to success on LinkedIn is twofold:

1. **Consistency.** Post daily. Yes, every single day including weekends. The algorithm favors those who are active. Plus, the more swings you take the more chances you have to hit a home run.

2. **Engagement.** Respond to comments, like relevant posts, engage in group conversations...all of these activities are essential if you want your posts to be seen by more people. If you're not engaging with your followers, they might just move on to the next person who did. Don't miss out on building those connections.

So, how do you achieve this?

Well, the key is to stay laser-focused when you post on LinkedIn every day. Don't try to be everything for. Instead, keep your posts tightly aligned with your target audience and their needs. Let's say you offer web design services for restaurants. Share some valuable tips on improving restaurant websites and driving online orders. Be the go-to resource in your niche, like we talked about in the chapter "How to Master Offer/Market Fit."

When you post daily, try to avoid being overly self-promotional. Don't make every post about your services or company. Of course, you can naturally discuss case studies and success stories, but make that the exception, not the rule. Focus more on providing genuinely valuable advice and education for your audience without constantly pushing your services. This nurturing approach helps build strong relationships.

Now, let's talk about engaging on LinkedIn. Make it a daily habit to set aside some time in your calendar to check notifications and comments. Join a few active groups in your industry and participate regularly. Like and comment on at least 5-10 posts from your target audience every day. These small but consistent actions add up over time and expand your reach. Just spending 15-20 minutes daily can make a significant difference in ensuring your regular posts get the visibility they deserve.

Lastly, why LinkedIn over Facebook, X, TikTok, and the likes?

LinkedIn is a game-changer for B2B agency owners. It's not like your typical social network—it's a powerhouse that helps you expand your reach and boost credibility. Trust me, with a hungry audience of professionals ready to connect with industry experts, you can establish yourself as an influential thought leader. Plus, the algorithm loves when you consistently post and engage in your niche. It's all about targeted networking and forging valuable partnerships. With its business focus, killer analytics, and lead generation tools, it's no brainer that LinkedIn should be the cornerstone of your social media presence as an agency owner. Show up, stay disciplined, and watch those dividends grow over time.

2. Create long form content

Long-form content becomes the driver for everything. If you can sit down each week and record a 20 minute video, you can turn that video into 10 short video clips for social media, 3 blog posts, a podcast episode and 5 LinkedIn posts.

Long-form content also builds authority and trust. If someone sits down to watch a 20 minute video, the likelihood of them remembering you and potentially becoming a lead are exponentially higher. Not to mention, long-form written content ranks incredibly well in search engines. Those meaty articles can drive organic traffic for months and years after publishing, compounding your ROI.

But it's not just about optics or algorithms. Long-form content showcases your ability to solve complex problems in depth. Every section adds another dimension to your expertise. That depth resonates far more than a brief social post or blog ever could.

Long-form content also provides lead magnets, protecting your sales funnel. Think about it - would you rather fill out a form to access a quick tip or template, or a comprehensive blueprint for dominating search marketing? No-brainer.

Here are a few suggestions to help you leverage long-form content:

- Research and create an in-depth guide on a topic important to your target clients. Aim for 5,000+ words.
- Extract key insights, examples or data points from the guide. Share these as condensed social media posts or blog updates to pique interest.

- Turn sections of the guide into short explainer videos. Post these natively on platforms like YouTube and LinkedIn.

- Promote the full, downloadable guide in your emails, ads and website. Use it as a lead magnet.

- Use the guide as source material for a webinar, workshop or podcast episode.

- Write a case study showcasing how the insights from the guide helped a client.

- Don't get bogged down perfecting details. Complete a solid draft, then refine.

- Include visual elements like charts, graphs and diagrams to engage readers.

- Update and improve the guide over time to keep it evergreen.

The long and short of it? Long-form content cuts through noise, builds authority, and converts leads. So don't shy away from length. Draft that 10,000 word guide. Create an epic case study. Give your audience value that keeps them hooked till the very last word.

3. Launch a VSL funnel

Video Sales Letters (VSLs) are the new age lead generation tactic for agencies that aren't afraid to go big. When I say big, I mean in terms of investment, ambition, and results. VSL funnels are not for agencies looking for small tweaks in their marketing.

This is a bold, aggressive generation campaign designed especially for those agencies that have a substantial amount of money to invest, with a singular goal: transform that money into profit.

The idea behind a VSL is simple, yet profound: create an engaging video that speaks directly to a potential client's pain points, offers a solution, and leads them down a sales funnel. But don't let its simplicity fool you; this is a high-stakes game with massive rewards.

Think of VSL as the faucet funnel. Just like a faucet, you turn it on when you need it, and you turn it off when you don't. The key here is not the actual source of traffic (though platforms like Meta, LinkedIn, or YouTube can be potent sources) but the content and the asset you provide.

Here's a breakdown of how to effectively launch your VSL funnel:

1. **Understand the Problem and Pain Points**: It's not about you or your agency; it's about them. What issues are your target audience grappling with? Be specific. Let's say you cater to law firms; maybe they're struggling with generating consistent leads from Google. That's your entry.

2. **Write The Script and Record The Video**: Create a video that addresses the pain point you've identified. This video should not just be about your agency's solutions, but about providing genuine value to your target audience. The trick here is to make them feel the weight of the problem (agitate it) and then present your solution as the remedy.

3. **Set Up the Funnel**: Just having a video isn't enough. Use platforms like ClickFunnels or Unbounce to create landing pages that guide leads through your funnel. Remember, the messaging should remain consistent throughout. A lead should feel like they're on a seamless journey, not a disjointed trip with jarring messaging changes.

4. **Optimize, Analyze, and Adapt**: Like any funnel, you'll need to invest in ads to drive traffic. Monitor your metrics closely. See what's working and what's not, and don't be afraid to adapt. For example, if LinkedIn ads are generating more qualified leads than Facebook, pivot your strategy accordingly.

5. **Have a Follow-Up Strategy**: A VSL funnel isn't just about getting leads but converting them. Ensure you have a clear follow-up strategy, whether that's email sequences, additional content, or direct outreach. Remember, nurturing is as essential as capturing.

6. **Invest Wisely**: This is not a low-budget strategy. As mentioned, it's for agencies ready to make a significant investment. But here's the thing: when done right, the ROI is tremendous. The key word here is "comfortably". If you can comfortably invest substantial sums into this strategy for a few months, and meticulously refine your approach based on data, you're in the game.

VSL is not for every agency out there. It's for the bold, the ambitious, and those ready to play in the big leagues. It's a cutting-edge strategy that, if mastered, can change the trajectory of your agency. But only if you're willing to put in the time, money, and effort required.

Action Steps for Mastering Client Acquisition

After diving deep into Pillar 4, you have gained a wealth of knowledge about client acquisition. Now, it's time to put that knowledge into practice. Here are actionable steps to help you translate your learnings into tangible results.

1. Clarify and Articulate Your Offer

Be crystal clear about what you offer and how it benefits your clients.

- *Write down in one sentence what your business offers.*

- *Convert that offer into a client-centric statement, showing the benefit to them. E.g., "We design websites" becomes "Get a website that turns visitors into customers."*

- *Post this benefit on your main social media platform today. Monitor the response.*

2. Develop Your Marketing Thesis

Communicate your unique value to your target audience.

- *Write a 1-2 sentence thesis summarizing your brand's viewpoint and value proposition.*

- *Create a mind map that breaks down this thesis into individual content topics or themes.*

- *Populate your content calendar with these topics, scheduling them out for the next month or quarter.*

3. Dive into Content Creation

Establish trust, authority, and a connection with potential clients.

- *Utilize frameworks like PAS, Before and After, or AIDA to guide the structure of your content.*

- *Produce the content, ensuring it aligns with your marketing thesis and addresses the pain points or needs of your audience.*

- *Schedule and publish this content on your chosen platforms, whether it's your blog, LinkedIn, or other channels.*

4. Implement a Proven Tactic

Choose one tactic to start with based on your resources and strengths.

- *LinkedIn: Commit to posting daily. Engage with comments, share insights, and interact with other posts to boost visibility.*

- *Long-Form Content: Identify a comprehensive topic and start drafting a detailed guide or article. Use the content to solidify your authority on the topic.*

- *VSL Funnel: Begin by scripting your video. Focus on a core pain point and how your services offer a solution. Set up a landing page and invest in promoting the VSL to your target audience.*

PILLAR 5

Sales

The final frontier of scaling an agency business - sales.

For agencies, the sales process can often feel like a bottomless pit. Proposals, follow ups, never-ending calls, prospects ghosting, deals falling through at the last minute – it's overwhelming.

In this chapter, we'll explore how to refine your sales methodology to scale your agency with simplicity. But first, let's address the elephant in the room – your role.

The Truth About You and Sales

If you're like most agency owners, you probably think you're the only person who can handle sales. You handle everything from discovery calls to closing deals, unwilling to relinquish control to anyone else. After all, no one understands your offer better than you, right?

But here's the hard truth: you can't call yourself a CEO if you're still doing sales on a daily basis.

Being indispensable often stems from distrust. You may hesitate to hand over sales, fearing missed nuances or bad impressions.

But the truth? Sales is a full-time job. It requires dedicated focus on building pipelines, nurturing leads, and guiding prospects. You simply can't provide that while also focusing on growth initiatives, team leadership, and service innovation. Attempting to wear all hats will only lead to mediocre results across the board.

That's why sales is the final frontier of scaling your agency. You can't scale your business if you're taking discovery calls, building proposals and chasing people down for decisions.

The hard truth is, you can't call yourself a "CEO" until you've pulled yourself out of sales completely.

The solution lies in shifting from sales reliance to sales enablement. You need to empower your team with the knowledge, strategies, and tools to carry the sales torch successfully.

This requires revamping your sales methodology to be simple, scalable, and not dependent on your direct involvement. Let's explore how to make that happen.

The "consultative" sales approach

A good agency sales representative should have two sets of core skills:

1. **Sales skills**: Adept at communication, possessing exceptional organization, and capable of making enticing offers that bring deals to close.

2. **Marketing skills**: Exhibiting consultative expertise, with a profound understanding of products/offers, and the ability to thoroughly analyze businesses.

Most sales professionals usually possess one or the other, and you usually end up in a situation where you handle sales because "no one else can do it better" than you.

The good news is there's a way to pull yourself out of sales without relying on finding "unicorn" sales reps. We just need to alter our approach and fix your sales process. The truth is that most agencies don't understand *how* to sell agency services and chances are you're one of them.

This is not a "Wolf Of Wall Street" approach to selling. Your goal is <u>not</u> to try and convince them to buy something they don't need by using persuasion tactics and hard closes. This approach doesn't work in agency sales, because sales cycles are longer because. There's a lot to consider before a prospect makes a decision - budgets, seasonality, relationships with existing agencies.

Instead, we want to lean into being an advisor, a consultant, a subject matter expert. In case you haven't picked up on it, there's a common theme inside this book that's all about solving your client's problems. In sales, your job is to demonstrate your understanding of their problem and present them with a solution.

With this approach, prospects view you as a trusted advisor rather than a sales rep. Conversations become more authentic, and you're able to establish a genuine connection.

Less hard closes, more deep conversations. Clients want to work with experts that they trust, not pushy sales people.

Here are some hallmarks of consultative sales approach:

- Asking thoughtful questions to understand needs and goals. Don't assume you have all the answers.

- Offering insights and ideas, not demands or ultimatums. Enable clients to arrive at solutions themselves.

- Avoiding industry jargon and over-the-top promises. Keep it real.

- Listening intently instead of dominating the discussion. Give them space to share freely.

- Establishing next steps collaboratively, not prescribed unilaterally. Make it a partnership.

Consultative selling requires patience and discipline. You may need to resist the urge to jump into promotions or proposals. But taking the time to listen, advise, and guide pays off with higher trust, stronger relationships, and more closed deals.

The core principles of agency sales

Before we get into the sales process, there's a few items I think are important to cover when thinking about sales for your agency.

- **Sales is a full time responsibility for *someone*.** There's a ton of work that goes into building an effective sales department, it's not just calls and proposals. If you treat sales like a part time activity, you will get part time results.

- **You're not selling services, you're selling results.** We covered this in detail in Chapters 1 and 2 in this book, but it's important to push it forward into your marketing and sales as well. You do not exist to sell a service, you exist to help your target client solve customer acquisition problems. The faster you can deliver results, the better.

- **Don't get emotional about deals.** This is just as much a life principle as it is for sales, but don't get emotionally invested into things that are completely outside of your control - it will beat you down overtime and sap your energy. Leads come and go, you are not going to close them all. *The best deal is always the next one.*

- **The role of marketing is to generate interest, the role of sales is to generate leads.** Too many sales specialists blame marketing when their pipeline is empty. Marketing's job is to create demand and interest in the marketplace, it's the role of sales to capture / harness / guide that demand into a qualified pipeline. That means using social media, outbound email / calls and networking to create deal flow.

The agency sales process

A lot of agencies don't have a formal, documented process for sales - this is a huge mistake. Having a process ensures you don't waste your time chasing down prospects that will never close and that nothing falls through the cracks.

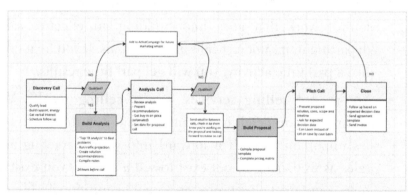

Can't see the process document? Head to theagencyblueprintbook.com to get FREE access to the process flow.

Our sales process is simple. It is grouped into 4 parts:

1. Discovery Call: The First Touchpoint

The goal of this call is to understand what the prospect's problem is, whether it's something we can solve and if they have the budget to do so. You want to weed out any mismatches early.

- **Objective**: Dive deep into the prospect's needs, budget, and timeline. Qualify the prospect to ensure they are worth spending more time on.

- **Before the Call**:
    - Do your homework. Research the prospect's company, industry, and any recent developments.
    - Draft a list of questions to uncover their challenges and aspirations.

- **The Call**:
    - Lock in a 30-minute Zoom session. Use tools like Calendly to make scheduling a breeze.
    - Qualify the lead with a series of questions to make sure they are a good fit.
    - Build rapport and good energy. Get verbal interest (so you don't waste your time).
    - Schedule the follow up while you are on the call.

- **Timeframe**: Set this up within 2 days of initial contact. Keep the ball rolling.

THEBLUEPRINT.TRAINING

Discovery Call Prep Template

This document is to help you stay on track with your sales calls. Use it to always have a series of questions and discussion points on hand, also use it to take notes (super important)!

- Date:
- Prospect name:
- Prospect email:
- Prospect phone:

Call prep notes

- Drop the website into a crawler (if time) and Ahrefs / SEMrush to get context for the site (1 - 3 recs)

- Review their website and take some initial notes on your thoughts. We're always thinking about issues + solutions during this time

- Over the last year, traffic seems to have fallen in half...reasons?

Discovery call template that we provide to our agency clients at The Blueprint Training.

2. Analysis Call: Rolling Up the Sleeves

This is the most time-consuming part of the sales process, so it's critically important that you qualify the lead. If they were lukewarm or not qualified, <u>do not do an analysis</u>. You will waste your time, your energy and burn yourself out.

- **Objective**: Complete an analysis that showcases to the prospect that you clearly understand the scope of their problem and you have a solution. The end of the call you should have buy-in to move the process to a proposal.

- **Before the Call**:

  - Conduct a comprehensive "Top 10" analysis of their website. Identify gaps, opportunities, and potential strategies to get them more customers.

- **The Call:**
  - Present your findings. Walk them through your insights and present your potential solution.
  - Engage in a two-way conversation. Ensure they grasp the implications and the transformative solutions you're proposing.
  - Discuss the estimated price tag and the possible ROI.
- **Timeframe**: Aim for 3-5 days post the discovery call. Give yourself time to prep, but don't let it drag. Next, send a check in email in-between calls, let them know you're working on the proposal and looking forward to meeting with them.

Deep Diving Into The "Top 10 Analysis"

This is such an important part of the "consultative" approach because this is your chance to sell with value. A large portion of time during the sales process should end up here, so let's spend some additional time breaking down what should go into what I like to call the "Top 10" analysis.

For an SEO analysis, The Top 10 analysis examines elements like:

- **Technical health** - how elements like site speed, metadata, and indexing impact performance.
- **Content assets** - the focus, depth, and interlinking of your existing content.
- **Link profile** - the quantity and quality of external sites linking to your domain.
- **Ranking analysis** - how you stack up for target keywords against competitors.

- **Site architecture** - the sitemap, page structure and internal linking.

- **Local optimization** - factors like GMB, reviews, citations and local content.

The goal of the analysis is to find areas of opportunity for a prospect - what avenues can you exploit to get them more customers, quickly? What errors can you fix that will lead to a quick turn around in traffic or performance? What are their competitors doing that you can learn from (and steal) to implement on the prospect's website?

A great analysis trumps a great sales pitch every time. A prospect wants to see that you understand and can solve their problems. The Top 10 Analysis is the perfect tool to communicate that.

This analysis culminates in a presentation on your second call, outlining the most pressing issues and biggest missed opportunities. Remember to bundle it up with data-backed recommendations on how you can capitalize on this intel.

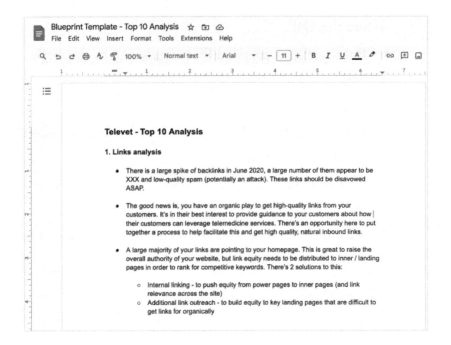

Analysis template we provide to clients inside The Blueprint Training

3. Proposal Call: Sealing the Deal

All parties must be present. Present a tailored, written proposal that outlines your process, timeline and pricing. Be prepared to address questions and concerns. Don't forget to clearly explain any strategies or options you're proposing and how they can benefit them in real terms. Make sure to include a few customer references, reviews or success.

- **Objective**: You should close a minimum of 50% of every proposal you send. If you find your close rate is lower than that, you did not properly qualify the prospect. Every proposal you send should have already gotten verbal buy-in from the prospect.

- **Before the Call:**
  - Put together a proposal that clearly details the scope of work, pricing, timeline and expected results.
- **The Call:**
  - Walk them through the proposal. Highlight the scope, pricing, deliverables, and timelines.
  - Address concerns, answer questions, and aim for a verbal agreement by the end.
  - **Timeframe**: Within a week of the analysis call. Strike while the iron's hot.

Proposal Deep Dive

Now, with the treasure trove of intel extracted from the Top 10 and traffic analyses, you have everything needed to craft a winning proposal.

Your proposal should distill your extensive research into an executive summary of:

- Summary of prospect's goals, challenges, and opportunities
- Presentation of Top 10 analysis and traffic projections
- Proposed solutions aligned to analysis, including detailed deliverables
- Pricing breakdown based on effort and resources required
- Timeframes and milestones
- Examples of clients you've helped and credentials
- Next steps and contact info

The goal of a proposal is to help the prospect shift from an analytical, research-focused mindset to envisioning real possibilities through partnering with you. You want to inspire them to imagine what their business could become by leveraging your expertise and proven strategies.

BONUS: The Traffic Projection Analysis

A key part of every proposal is answering the question…

"What can I expect as a result from working with you?"

Most agencies glaze over this, and it's a reason why your close rate is so low. If you want to close more deals, you have to forecast results for them. Otherwise, what are they paying for?

Leveraging tools like SEMrush or Ahrefs, analyze the current traffic, competitors' traffic, keyword difficulty, etc. Try to forecast the lift you could see through:

- Improving existing page rankings
- Targeting new high-value keywords
- Boosting domain authority via links

The projections provide a tangible way for prospects to understand the possible impact your services can drive. Aim to present multiple scenarios reflecting different effort levels, from conservative to aggressive, to give prospects options.

We built a custom tool that handles all the heavy lifting for you and builds forecasts for proposals, you can check it out to leverage in your next proposal -> www.trafficprojection.com

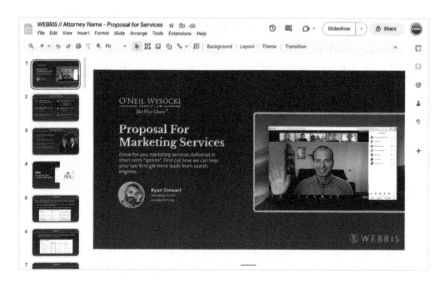

Proposal template we give to clients inside The Blueprint Training.

4. Close and Onboard: The Home Stretch

This is where a lot of agencies lose their minds. You have a great discovery call, a productive review of your analysis, a verbal "yes" on your proposal…then silence. The prospect completely "ghosts" you right when you think they are going to close.

The key to avoiding this is to hold the prospect accountable for the time they've taken. Set dates, use those dates to follow up aggressively.

- **Objective**: Transition prospect into paying client with effective, timely communications.

- **What to do**:

  - At the end of each call, you must set a date for the next action.

- For example, on the discovery call, set the date for the analysis call while still on the discovery call.

- On the analysis call, set the date for the proposal call, while still on the analysis call.

- On the proposal call, set an expected decision date. When you set these dates, you hold them accountable, which gives you the freedom to follow up with a purpose, instead of chasing them endlessly.

- If you find yourself in a situation where you're emailing them non stop ("just bumping this up"), give them a final offer and move on. They will come back when ready, but it's not worth your energy to chase them around.

- Closure:
  - Once you get the green light, send over an agreement to sign and an invoice. Do not move forward until the agreement is signed and the invoice is paid!

- Onboarding:
  - Hand them over to the client services team. Within the same day, the prospect should get an onboarding email with instructions to get started with your services. This email should include onboarding questions, how to get your team the necessary accesses, and a link to schedule an onboarding call.

  - The first week is critical. You need to make sure you're showing the client the right attention so they don't get buyers remorse and back out.

- **Timeframe**: Aim to seal the deal within 5 days of the proposal. If they're dragging their feet, don't waste time chasing them down. Your energy is better spent on prospects who are ready to make a decision.

Action Steps for Mastering Sales

After exploring the sales process and strategies in Pillar 5, it's time to put these learnings into practice. Use the following exercises to transform your sales approach from chaotic to streamlined.

1. Define Your Sales Process

Visualize the journey from lead to customer (or just use ours - discovery, analysis, proposal, close).

2. Prepare Discovery Documents

Do your homework on your prospect before the initial call to make sure you're building the right rapport and qualifying the lead.

3. Develop Your Analysis Framework

The most important part of your pitch is demonstrating your knowledge and acumen. We like to use a "Top 10 Analysis" framework that ensures every pitch gets the right attention and we're always driving towards solving that prospect's problem.

4. Build a Proposal Template

Once they buy into the strategy you present in the analysis, a proposal covers the scope, priving, timelines, deliverables and expected results. This can be a template, as the analysis is the custom work part of this process.

5. Set Clear Next Steps and Follow-Ups

Guide prospects smoothly through sales stages by confirming next steps and timelines at the end of every sales call.

6. Track and Optimize Performance

Use a CRM to track deals, open action items and overall performance. This will allow you to analyze any leaks in your sales process and improve conversion rates. At minimum, you should never be closing less than 30% of your proposals. If you are, you have a major issue with your pitch or the quality of your leads.

Making the leap

This knowledge in this book took me 15 years to acquire, and almost 3 years to write.

So why am I willing to give this all away for just the cost of a book?

Because information alone is worthless – execution is everything. I know most people who read this book will nod along with the concepts yet take no real action.

We're plagued by a disease of constant content consumption with no application. Endless scrolling of social feeds, reading content that provides little value, always looking at what others are doing but never taking steps ourselves.

It's so easy to fall into this trap. The torrent of information online makes us feel productive because we're ingesting so much. But at the end of the day, they're empty calories that don't translate into results.

This book is your wake-up call. A blueprint for tangible change.

I've laid out a clear path to transform your agency, regardless of where you're starting. For those running an existing agency, these strategies will help you find greater profitability and success. For those looking to start, this is a proven model that works.

But knowledge alone is not enough. You need to take action.

So where to begin?

Start by reviewing the core concepts and identifying 1-2 key areas you want to implement first. Don't try to overhaul everything at once. Focus on small wins.

For instance, you could start by refining your positioning and offer for a target niche. Or you could spend a month perfecting your sales methodology. Master that first milestone fully before moving to the next.

Momentum fuels motivation. By seeing positive outcomes from initial steps, you'll gain the confidence boost needed to continue implementing further changes.

Next, get clear on your timeline and milestones. Plot out what you want to accomplish in the next week, month, quarter. Having defined goals and deadlines will help ensure you stay on track amidst the hustle of agency work. Print out your plan and schedule time to work on it.

Speaking of time, block out dedicated slots for strategic work. Don't just wait for "free" time to appear. Take command of your calendar. If you schedule it, it's more likely to happen. Protect those blocks from client calls or other reactive work.

Involve your team. Present your vision, timeline, and goals. Get their buy-in. Brainstorm and collaborate to determine how each person can contribute. When everyone has clarity and purpose, execution becomes smoother.

Check your mindset as you embark on this journey. Be aware of self-limiting beliefs that could be holding you back. Thoughts like "this seems hard" or "maybe this won't work for us" will undermine your efforts. Catch and reframe these thoughts when they arise.

Next, celebrate small wins. Mark milestones with team lunches or shoutouts. Seeing progress will keep you motivated to stay the course when obstacles hit. And they will hit - change isn't always comfortable as we step out of old ways. Recognize that discomfort is a sign you're stretching your abilities. View setbacks as data points, not failures.

Leverage communities and courses as needed. You don't have to go it alone. There are spaces like The Blueprint Training with agency experts who can provide guidance and support. But use these wisely to supplement your efforts, not replace them.

Review and reassess regularly. Each month, examine what's working well and what's not. Adapt your approach based on results and feedback. Refinement is key to sustaining an effective strategy.

The final step? Don't stop once you check items off your list. *Continual improvement is the key to long-term success.* Build in regular time to re-evaluate, optimize and keep your agency at the cutting edge.

The knowledge within these pages contains immense potential to transform your agency, but only if put into consistent action. Avoid complacency once you've seen some progress. Mastery requires lifelong learning and evolution.

The journey ahead requires commitment, resilience, and a willingness to step outside your comfort zone. The path may not always be smooth, but the horizon is bright for those who press forward.

Within these pages lies a blueprint crafted to guide you toward that horizon. One where your agency operates at peak performance, your clients view you as an invaluable asset, and your vision comes into sharp focus.

Take this knowledge, combine it with consistent action, and enable your agency to ascend to new heights. Not just for a season, but for the long-haul. For when you commit to lifelong learning and continued evolution, mastery will follow.

> *The ball is now in your court. I've laid the foundation - it's up to you to build upon it.*

Keep this book nearby as a reference as you move forward. Highlight key passages, bookmark pivotal concepts. Most importantly, open it frequently. Use it as fuel to spark motivation when obstacles arise.

Remember, true success is not achieved overnight. But if you stay the course, victory awaits around the bend. I look forward to hearing of your wins, lessons, and moments of transformation.

You made it! We'd love to discuss how we can help your agency implement the teachings laid out in this book. You can learn more about partnering up with us at https://theblueprint.training/

Made in the USA
Las Vegas, NV
20 November 2023

81209834R10066